Readers Respond to

Revolution
in World Missions

"I have just read *Revolution in World Missions*. This book greatly ministered to me and stirred me in a way no book has ever done. How can we order more copies?"

—Pastor J.P., Lakeside, Oregon

"I was a missionary in Nigeria for 20 years and understand what this book is all about."

—Mrs. D.T., Kearney, Arizona

"Your book stirred me to tears and drove me to prayer! Please send me more information about your ministry to native missionaries. May God continue to bless you and use you."

—Miss J.S., Towson, Maryland

"I read your book and think it is one of the most dynamic, down-to-earth books that I have ever read. I want to give a copy to our pastor, each board member and selected other people at our church."

—Mr. P.W., Santa Margarita, California

"I just finished reading *Revolution in World Missions* by K.P. Yohannan. The thought that for the cost of supporting one missionary from Canada as many as 10 local Asian missionaries could be supported continues to astound me."

—Mr. S.D., Calgary, Alberta

"We both read K.P.'s book and were very moved to change part of our lifestyle to further the Gospel. I hope we can do more as we get braver!"

—Mr. and Mrs. D.F., Los Alamos, New Mexico

"I saw myself too many times in your book, K.P. Although we are going through a financial trial right now, I realize how very blessed we are compared to most of the rest of the world. I have caught sight of your vision."

—Mrs. S.S., Chesapeake, Virginia

"After finishing your book, our family is now deciding how we can be a part of God's plan for His Church in Asia. If you have any suggestions, we would enjoy your input—especially from the experience you have acquired."

—Mr. P.P., Fort Atkinson, Wisconsin

"We have been challenged and convicted by *Revolution in World Missions.* We believe that our Lord Jesus is offering us the chance to share in His work in Asia—a chance we don't want to miss!"

—Mr. and Mrs. M.D., Pacifica, California

"After reading *Revolution in World Missions,* I am convinced our small amount of money can do more good in this mission than many others we participate in."

—Mrs. I.T., Houston, Texas

WHAT INTERNATIONAL CHRISTIAN LEADERS ARE SAYING ABOUT

 GOSPEL FOR ASIA

"There are many that talk a good message, but not too many who actually live it out. Gospel for Asia is serious about the challenge of reaching unreached people groups. . . . The 10/40 Window is where the Gospel needs to go. And GFA is a major force today standing in the gap. They represent the primary unreached peoples on planet Earth. GFA has what it takes to penetrate the 10/40 Window."

—LUIS BUSH, Director, World Inquiry

"Gospel for Asia has become one of the more significant pioneer missionary agencies, with a good accountability structure. . . . They are doing an excellent job."

—PATRICK JOHNSTONE, Author, *Operation World*

"Gospel for Asia is not a movement, but a phenomenon. GFA has become one of the most significant mission organizations of this century."

—GEORGE VERWER, Founder and former International Director, Operation Mobilization

"Every once in a while God gives to His people a man who is qualified to cut us open, give us a diagnosis and prescribe a remedy for our healing. K.P. Yohannan is such a man. K.P. is impatient with intellectual knowledge unless it translates into holy living and a single-minded determination to see the Church around the world grow for the glory of God. And he practices what he preaches. If you listen to him carefully, you will leave with eternity stamped on your heart."

—ERWIN LUTZER, Senior Pastor,
Moody Church, Chicago, IL

"Although there are many fine Christian groups working worldwide, I've found Gospel for Asia to be unique. A very small amount of money can fully support an evangelist to effectively present Jesus Christ to eager listeners abroad. I have worked with these men . . . and have learned from the values of commitment and wholesale dedication. K.P. Yohannan lives and breathes integrity. This integrity has filtered to the very fiber of his ministry. I am honored to be a partner with GFA."

—SKIP HEITZIG, Senior Pastor, Ocean Hills
Community Church, San Juan Capistrano, CA

"K.P. Yohannan leads one of the largest, if not the largest missionary movement, working across the nation of India in evangelism and church-planting work. As Gospel for Asia has grown and established itself, the ministry has become balanced and is now involved in a host of cooperative efforts with other mission agencies. The impact of GFA's ministry in India is very significant, especially in their evangelistic training, radio and church-planting work."

—JOSEPH D'SOUZA, Executive Director,
Operation Mobilization India

"To open their eyes, and to turn them from darkness to light, and from the power of Satan unto God, that they may receive forgiveness of sins, and inheritance among them which are sanctified by faith that is in me."

Acts 26:18

Revolution
in World Missions

K.P. Yohannan

BOOKS

a division of Gospel for Asia

www.gfa.org

ISBN: 1-59589-001-7

Published by gfa books, a division of Gospel for Asia
1800 Golden Trail Court
Carrollton, TX 75010 USA
phone: (972) 300-7777
fax: (972) 300-7778

Printed in the United States of America

First printing, July 1986	*Sixteenth printing, March 1997*
Second printing, November 1986	*Seventeenth printing, July 1997*
Third printing, May 1987	*Eighteenth printing, January 1998*
Fourth printing, December 1987	*Nineteenth printing, August 1998*
Fifth printing, July 1989	*Twentieth printing, November 1998*
Sixth printing, May 1991	*Twenty-first printing, March 2000*
Seventh printing, January 1992	*Twenty-second printing, April 2001*
Eighth printing, June 1992	*Twenty-third printing, November 2001*
Ninth printing, August 1993	*Twenty-fourth printing, June 2002*
Tenth printing, March 1994	*Twenty-fifth printing, October 2002*
Eleventh printing June 1994	*Twenty-sixth printing, May 2003*
Twelfth printing, March 1995	*Twenty-seventh printing, October 2003*
Thirteenth printing, October 1995	*Twenty-eighth printing, March 2004*
Fourteenth printing, May 1996	*Twenty-ninth printing, July 2004*
Fifteenth printing, October 1996	*Thirtieth printing, December 2004*

For more information about other materials, visit our website www.gfa.org.

*This book is dedicated to George Verwer, founder and
former international director of Operation Mobilization, whom
the Lord used to call me into the ministry and
whose life and example have influenced me more
than any other single individual's.*

Contents

Foreword

We all are skeptical of Christians with big dreams. We don't know why exactly—perhaps we have met too many who pursued visions but whose personal lives were nightmares.

The first time we remember meeting K.P. Yohannan we brought him home for dinner, and our family dragged this slight Indian along with us to a high school gymnasium to sit through an American rite of passage—an all-school spaghetti supper. Across the paper tablecloth, the garlic bread and the centerpieces—shellacked lunch sacks filled with an assortment of dried weeds and pasta (created by members of the Mains family!)—we heard of a dream to win not only India but all of Asia for Christ.

Since that evening in the noisy gymnasium in West Chicago, Illinois, there have been many more shared experiences—phone calls from Dallas; trips to the cities and backwaters of India; pastors' conferences in open thatched-roofed, bamboo-sided pavilions; laughter; travel on Two-Thirds World roads; and times of prayer.

Very simply said, we have come to believe in K.P.

And we believe in his plan for evangelization that, with the profundity of simplicity, bypasses the complexity of technology and challenges Asians to give up their lives to win their fellow countrymen to Christ.

This book, *Revolution in World Missions*, reveals one of God's master plans to reach the world before the end of time. With absolute confidence we know we can endorse the integrity of its author, a man of God, and we are thrilled with the work of Gospel for Asia.

You can read knowing that those evangelists traveling into the unreached villages of Asia have more heart, more fervor, more passion to spread the Gospel of Christ than most of us who are surrounded by the comforts and conveniences of our Western world.

We know because we have seen them and talked with them, and they have put us to shame.

Internationals are the new wave of the missionary effort. K.P. Yohannan's book paints the picture of how that dream is becoming reality.

This is one dreamer of whom we are no longer skeptical. We think you will find reason to believe as well.

David and Karen Mains

Acknowledgments

Hundreds of people have had an impact on this volume—from those who have made suggestions, to those who have given encouragement, to those who have influenced my life and ministry. I want to thank all of them—and all of you—and thank the Lord for placing you in my path.

Of those especially close to me during the long writing, editing and review of this manuscript, I would like to thank David and Karen Mains and Gayle Erwin for their honest criticism and unwavering support of this entire project. Special thanks also are due Margaret Jordan, Heidi Chupp and Katie McCall, who typed the manuscript. And thanks to my secretary, Teresa Chupp, and her assistants, for their hard work in this updated edition. Thanks.

And my special thanks to Bob Granholm, former executive director of Frontiers in Canada, for his suggestions for the revision that helped bring balance and clear up misunderstanding.

Most of all, of course, my greatest debt is to my wife, Gisela, for her careful reading and for suggestions that made the critical difference in several passages. Her emotional and spiritual support made the writing of this book possible. Without her standing beside me and encouraging me during these eventful years, this book—and the message it proclaims—would not have been possible.

Introduction

Before the second half of the 1980s rolled around, most evangelical Christians in Western countries tended to view mission history in terms of only two great waves of activity.

The first wave broke over the New Testament world in the first century as the apostles obeyed the Great Commission. It swept through the Jewish and pagan communities of the Roman Empire, bringing the message of salvation to all of the Mediterranean world, much of southern Europe and even some parts of Asia.

The second wave was most often dated from William Carey's pioneer work in 18th-century India. It began a flood of 19th- and 20th-century missions to the colonies of the great European powers. Although World War II marked the end of this colonial era, it still frequently defines the image of missions for many Western Christians.

But around the world today, the Holy Spirit is breaking over Asian and African nations, raising up a new army of missionaries. Thousands of dedicated men and women are bringing the salvation story to their own people—millions of lost souls in closed countries who would probably never learn about the love of God by any other means. These humble, obscure pioneers of the Gospel are taking up the banner of the cross where colonial-era missions left off. They are the third wave of mission history—the native missionary movement.

As Christians in the West gradually develop a greater understanding of what this third wave means to world evangelism, we feel a potent challenge to our attitudes and lifestyles. Thousands of individuals and churches are praying for and supporting native missionaries on the frontiers of faith.

Revolution in World Missions has undergone various revisions over the years. I have sought to clarify basic areas of misunderstanding surrounding the native missionary movement, such as the changing role of Western missionaries and standards of accountability in native missions.

The impact of this book continues to grow. Pastors have written us, testifying of the dramatic changes their church's mission programs have had. Fathers and mothers—and their children—are learning to live more simply and creatively in order to support native missionaries. Young adults, faced with eternal matters, are choosing to make their lives count for the kingdom rather than succumb to the climb up the ladder.

I believe we will see this generation reached for Christ as this exciting third wave of mission leadership unites with concerned Christians, churches and mission agencies around the world. As we draw nearer to Christ in unity, feeling His heartbeat for lost and dying souls, we realize that we are all serving one King and one kingdom. May this book serve to bring greater unity and cooperation among all God's people, as we seek to obey His will together.

One

Only the Beginning

The silence of the great hall in Cochin was broken only by soft, choking sobs. The Spirit of God was moving over the room with awesome power—convicting of sin and calling men and women into His service. Before the meeting ended, 120 of the 1,200 pastors and Christian leaders present made their way to the altar, responding to the "call of the North."

They were not saying, "I'm willing to go," but rather "I am going."

They made the choice to leave home, village and family, business or career and go where they would be hated and feared. Meanwhile, another 600 pastors pledged to return to their congregations and raise up more missionaries who would leave South India and go to the North.

I stood silently in the holy hush, praying for the army of God crowded around the altar. I was humbled by the presence of God.

As I prayed, my heart ached for these men who came to the altar. How many would be beaten and go hungry or be cold and lonely in the years ahead? How many would sit in jails for their faith? I prayed for the blessing and protection of God on them—and for more sponsors across the seas to stand with them.

They were leaving material comforts, family ties and personal ambitions. Ahead lay a new life among strangers. But I also knew they would witness spiritual victory as many thousands turned to Christ and helped form new congregations in the unreached villages of North India.

With me in the meeting was U.S. Christian radio broadcaster David Mains, a serious student of revival. He had joined us in Cochin as one of the conference speakers. He later testified how the Lord had taken over the meeting in a most unusual way.

"It would hardly have been different," he wrote later, "had Jesus Himself been bodily among us. The spirit of worship filled the hall. The singing was electrifying. The power of the Holy Spirit came upon the audience. Men actually groaned aloud. I have read of such conviction in early American history during times like the two Great Awakenings, but I had never anticipated experiencing it firsthand."

But the Lord is not simply calling out a huge army of native workers. God is at work saving people from sin in numbers we never before dreamed possible. People are coming to Christ all across Asia at an accelerated rate wherever salvation is being proclaimed. In some areas—like India, Indonesia, the Philippines and Thailand—it is not uncommon now for the Christian community to grow as much in only one month as it formerly did in a whole year.

Reports of mass conversion and church growth are being underplayed in the Western press. The exciting truth about God's working in Asia has yet to be told, partly because the press has limited access. Except in a few countries, like Korea and the Philippines, the real story is not getting out.

Typical of the many native missionary movements that have sprung up overnight is the work of a brother from South India—a former military officer who gave up a commission and army career to help start a Gospel team in North India. He now leads more than 400 full-time missionaries.

Like other native mission leaders, he has discipled 10 "Timothys" who are directing the work in almost military precision. Each of them in turn will be able to lead dozens of additional workers who will have their own disciples.

With his wife he set an apostolic pattern for their workers similar to that of the apostle Paul. On one evangelistic tour that lasted 53 days, he and his family traveled by bullock cart and foot into some of the most backward areas of the tribal districts of Orissa state. There, working in the intense heat among people whose lifestyle is so primitive that it can be described only as animalistic, he saw hundreds converted. Throughout the journey, demons were cast out and miraculous physical healings took place daily. Thousands of the tribals—who were enslaved to idols and spirit-worship—heard the Gospel eagerly.

In just one month, he formed 15 groups of converts into new churches and assigned native missionaries to stay behind and build them up in the faith.

Similar miraculous movements are starting in almost every state of India and throughout other nations of Asia.

Native missionary Jesu Das was horrified when he first visited one village and found no believers there. The people were all worshiping hundreds of different gods, and four pagan priests controlled them through their witchcraft.

Stories were told of how these priests could kill people's cattle with witchcraft and destroy their crops. People were suddenly taken ill and died without explanation. The destruction and bondage the villagers were living in are hard to imagine. Scars, decay and death marked their faces, because they were totally controlled by the powers of darkness.

When Jesu Das told them about Christ, it was the first time they ever heard of a God who did not require sacrifices and offerings to appease His anger. As Jesu Das continued to preach in the marketplace, many people came to know the Lord.

But the priests were outraged. They warned Jesu Das that if he did not leave the village, they would call on their gods to kill him, his wife and their children. Jesu Das did not leave. He continued to preach, and villagers continued to be saved.

Finally, after a few weeks, the witch doctors came to Jesu Das and asked him the secret of his power.

"This is the first time our power did not work," they told him. "After doing the *pujas*, we asked the spirits to go and kill your family. But the spirits came back and told us they could not approach you or your family because you were always surrounded by fire. Then we called more powerful spirits to come after you—but they too returned, saying not only were you surrounded by fire, but angels were also around you all the time."

Jesu Das told them about Christ. The Holy Spirit convicted each of them of their sin of following demons and of the judgment to come. With tears, they repented, renouncing their gods and idols, and received Jesus Christ as Lord. As a result, hundreds of other villagers were set free from sin and bondage.

Through an indigenous organization in Thailand, where more than 200 native missionaries are doing pioneer village evangelism, one group personally shared their faith with 10,463 people in two months. Of these, 171 gave their lives to Christ, and six new churches were formed. More than 1,000 came to Christ in the same reporting period. Remember, this great harvest is happening in a Buddhist nation that never has seen such results.

Documented reports like these come to us daily from native teams in almost every Asian nation. But I am convinced these are only the first few drops of revival rain. In order to make the necessary impact, we must send out hundreds of thousands more workers. We are no longer praying for the proverbial "showers of blessings." Instead I am believing God for virtual thunderstorms of blessings in the days ahead.

How I became a part of this astonishing spiritual renewal in Asia is what this book is all about. And it all began with the prayers of a simple village mother.

Two

"O God, Let One of My Boys Preach!"

Achyamma's eyes stung with salty tears. But they were not from the cooking fire or the hot spices that wafted up from the pan. She realized time was short. Her six sons were growing beyond her influence. Yet not one showed signs of going into the Gospel ministry.

Except for the youngest—little "Yohannachan" as I was known—every one of her children seemed destined for secular work. My brothers seemed content to live and work around our native village of Niranam in Kerala, South India.

"O God," she prayed in despair, "let just one of my boys preach!" Like Hannah and so many other saintly mothers in the Bible, my mother had dedicated her children to the Lord. That morning, while preparing breakfast, she vowed to fast secretly until God called one of her sons into His service. Every Friday for the next three and a half years, she fasted. Her prayer was always the same.

But nothing happened. Finally, only I, scrawny and little—the baby of the family—was left. There seemed little chance I would preach. Although I had stood up in an evangelistic meeting at age eight, I was shy and timid and kept my faith mostly to myself. I showed no leadership skills and avoided sports and school functions. I was comfortable on the edge of village and family life, a shadowy figure who moved in and out of the scene almost unnoticed.

Then, when I was 16, my mother's prayers were answered. A visiting Gospel team from Operation Mobilization came to our church to present the challenge of faraway North India. My 90-pound frame strained to catch every word as the team spoke and showed slides of the North.

They told of stonings and beatings they received while preaching Christ in the non-Christian villages of Rajasthan and Bihar on the hot, arid plains of North India. Sheltered from contact with the rest of India by the high peaks of the Western Ghats, the lush jungles of Kerala on the Malabar Coast were all I knew of my homeland. And the Malabar Coast had long nourished India's oldest Christian community, begun when the flourishing sea trade with the Persian Gulf made it possible for St. Thomas to introduce Jesus Christ at nearby Cranagore in A.D. 52. Other Jews already were there, having arrived 200 years earlier. The rest of India seemed an ocean away to the Malayalam-speaking people of the southwest coast, and I was no exception.

As the Gospel team portrayed the desperately lost condition of the rest of the country—500,000 villages without a Gospel witness—I felt a strange sorrow for the lost. That day I vowed to help bring the Good News of Jesus Christ to those strange and mysterious states to the North. At the challenge to "forsake all and follow Christ," I somewhat rashly took the leap, agreeing to join the student group for a short summer crusade in unreached parts of North India.

My decision to go into the ministry largely resulted from my mother's faithful prayers. Although I still had not received what I later understood to be my real call from the Lord, my mother encouraged me to follow my heart in the matter. When I announced my decision, she wordlessly handed over 25 rupees—enough for my train ticket. I set off to apply to the mission's headquarters in Trivandrum.

There I got my first rebuff. Because I was underage, the mission's directors at first refused to let me join the teams going north. But I was permitted to attend the annual training conference to be held in Bangalore, Karnataka. At the conference I first heard missionary statesman George Verwer, who challenged me as never before to commit myself to a life of breathtaking, radical discipleship. I was impressed with how Verwer put the will of God for the lost world before career, family and self.

Alone that night in my bed, I argued with both God and my own conscience. By two o'clock in the morning, my pillow wet with sweat and tears, I shook with fear. What if God asked me to preach in the streets? How would I ever be able to stand up in public and speak? What if I were stoned and beaten?

I knew myself only too well. I could hardly bear to look a friend in the eye during a conversation, let alone speak publicly to hostile crowds on behalf of God. As I spoke the words, I realized that I was behaving as Moses did when he was called.

Suddenly, I felt that I was not alone in the room. A great sense of love and of my being loved filled the place. I felt the presence of God and fell on my knees beside the bed.

"Lord God," I gasped in surrender to His presence and will, "I'll give myself to speak for You—but help me to know that You're with me."

In the morning, I awoke to a world and people suddenly different. As I walked outside, the Indian street scenes looked the same as before: Children ran between the legs of people and cows, pigs and chickens wandered about, vendors carried baskets of bright fruit and flowers on their heads. I loved them all with a supernatural, unconditional love I'd never felt before. It was as if God had removed my eyes and replaced them with His so I could see people as the heavenly Father sees them—lost and needy but with potential to glorify and reflect Him.

I walked to the bus station. My eyes filled with tears of love. I knew that these people were all going to hell—and I knew God did not want them to go there. Suddenly I had such a burden for these masses that I had to stop and lean against a wall just to keep my balance. This was it: I knew I was feeling the burden of love God feels for the lost multitudes of India. His loving heart was pounding within mine, and I could hardly breathe. The tension was great. I paced back and forth restlessly to keep my knees from knocking in fright.

"Lord!" I cried. "If You want me to do something, say it, and give me courage."

Looking up from my prayer, I saw a huge stone. I knew immediately I had to climb that stone and preach to the crowds in the bus station. Scrambling up, I felt a force like 10,000 volts of electricity shooting through my body.

I began by singing a simple children's chorus. It was all I knew. By the time I finished, a crowd stood at the foot of the rock. I had not prepared myself to speak, but all at once God took over and filled my mouth with words of His love. I preached the Gospel to the poor as Jesus commanded His disciples to do. As the authority and power of God flowed through me, I had superhuman boldness. Words came out I never knew I had—and with a power clearly from above.

Others from the Gospel teams stopped to listen. The question of my age and calling never came up again. That was 1966, and I continued moving with mobile evangelistic teams for the next seven years. We traveled all over North India, never staying very long in any one village. Everywhere we went I preached in the streets while others distributed books and tracts. Occasionally, in smaller villages, we witnessed from house to house.

My urgent, overpowering love for the village people of India and the poor masses grew with the years. People even began to nickname me "Gandhi Man" after the father of modern India, Mahatma Gandhi. Like him, I realized without being told that if India were to be won, it would be by brown-skinned natives who loved the village people.

As I studied the Gospels, it became clear to me that Jesus understood well the principle of reaching the poor. He avoided the major cities, the rich, the famous and the powerful, concentrating His ministry on the poor laboring class. If we reach the poor, we have touched the masses of Asia.

As I traveled, viewing the effects of pagan religions on India, I realized that the masses of India are starving because they are slaves to sin. The battle against hunger and poverty is really a spiritual battle, not a physical or social one as secularists would have us believe.

The only weapon that will ever effectively win the war against disease, hunger, injustice and poverty in Asia is the Gospel of Jesus Christ. To look into the sad eyes of a hungry child or see the wasted life of a drug addict is to see only the evidence of Satan's hold on this world. All bad things are his handiwork. He is the ultimate enemy of mankind, and he will do everything within his considerable power to kill and destroy human beings. Fighting this powerful enemy with physical weapons is like fighting an armored tank with stones.

I can never forget one of the more dramatic encounters we had with these demonic powers. It was a hot and unusually humid day in 1970. We were preaching in the northwestern state of Rajasthan—the "desert of kings."

As was our practice before a street meeting, my seven coworkers and I stood in a circle to sing and clap hands to the rhythm of Christian folk songs. A sizeable crowd gathered, and I began to speak in Hindi, the local language. Many heard the Gospel for the first time and eagerly took our Gospels and tracts to read.

One young man came up to me and asked for a book to read. As I talked to him, I sensed in my spirit that he was hungry to know God. When we got ready to climb aboard our Gospel van, he asked to join us.

As the van lurched forward, he cried and wailed. "I am a terrible sinner," he shrieked. "How can I sit among you?" With that he started to jump from the moving van. We held on to him and forced him to the floor to prevent injury.

That night he stayed at our base and the next morning joined us for the prayer meeting. While we were praising and interceding, we heard a sudden scream. The young man was lying on the ground, tongue lolling out of his mouth, his eyes rolled back.

As Christians in a pagan land, we knew immediately he was demon-possessed. We gathered around him and began taking authority over the forces of hell as they spoke through his mouth.

"We are 74 of us. . . . For the past seven years we have made him walk barefoot all over India. He is ours. . . . " They spoke on, blaspheming and cursing, challenging us and our authority.

But as three of us prayed, the demons could not keep their hold on the young man. They came out when we commanded them to leave in the name of Jesus.

Sundar John was delivered, gave his life to Jesus and was baptized. Later he went to Bible college for two years. Since then the Lord has enabled him to teach and preach to thousands of people about Christ. Several native Indian churches have started as a result of his remarkable ministry—all from a man many people would have locked up in an insane asylum. And there are literally millions of people like him in India—deceived by demons and enslaved to their horrible passions and lusts.

This kind of miracle kept me going from village to village for those seven years of itinerant preaching. Our lives read like pages from the book of Acts. Most nights we slept between villages in roadside ditches, where we were relatively safe. Sleeping in non-Christian villages would expose us to many dangers. Our team always created a stir, and at times we even faced stonings and beatings.

The mobile Gospel teams I worked with—and often led—were just like family to me. I began to enjoy the gypsy lifestyle we lived and the total abandonment to the cause of Christ that is demanded of an itinerant evangelist. We were persecuted, hated and despised. Yet we kept going, knowing that we were blazing a trail for the Gospel in districts that had never before experienced an encounter with Christ.

One such village was Bhundi in Rajasthan. This was the first place I was beaten and stoned for preaching the Gospel. Often literature was destroyed. It seemed that mobs always were on the watch for us, and six times our street meetings were broken up. Our team leaders began to work elsewhere, avoiding Bhundi as much as possible. Three years later, a new team of native missionaries moved into the area under different leadership and preached again at this busy crossroads town.

Almost as soon as they arrived, one man began tearing up literature and grabbed a 19-year-old missionary, Alex Sam, by the throat. Although beaten severely, Sam knelt in the street and prayed for the salvation of souls in that hateful city.

"Lord," he prayed, "I want to come back here and serve You in Bhundi. I'm willing to die here, but I want to come back and serve You in this place."

Many older Christian leaders advised him against his decision, but being determined, he went back and rented a small room. Shipments of literature arrived, and he preached in the face of many difficulties. Today more than 100 people meet in a small church there. Those who persecuted us at one time now worship the Lord Jesus, as was the case with the apostle Paul.

This is the kind of commitment and faith it takes to win North Indian villages to the Lord Jesus.

One time we arrived in a town at daybreak to preach. But

word already had gone ahead from the nearby village where we had preached the day before.

As we had morning tea in a roadside stall, the local militant leader approached me politely. In a low voice that betrayed little emotion, he spoke:

"Get on your truck and get out of town in five minutes, or we'll burn it and you with it."

I knew he was serious. He was backed by a menacing crowd. Although we did "shake the dust from our feet" that day, today a church meets in that same village. In order to plant the Gospel, we must take risks.

For months at a time I traveled the dusty roads in the heat of the day and shivered through cold nights—suffering just as thousands of native missionaries are suffering today to bring the Gospel to the lost. In future years I would look back on those seven years of village evangelism as one of the greatest learning experiences of my life. We walked in Jesus' steps, incarnating and representing Him to masses of people who had never before heard the Gospel.

I was living a frenetic, busy life—too busy and thrilled with the work of the Gospel to think much about the future. There was always another campaign just ahead. But I was about to reach a turning point.

Three

The Seeds of Future Change

In 1971 I was invited to spend one month in Singapore at a new institute that had been started by John Haggai. It was still in the formative stages then—a place where Asian church leaders would be trained and challenged to witness for Christ.

Haggai was full of stories. In them all, Christians were overcomers and giants—men and women who received a vision from God and refused to let go of it. Diligence to your calling was a virtue to be highly prized.

Haggai was the first person who made me believe that nothing is impossible with God. And in Haggai I found a man who refused to accept impossibilities. The normal boundaries others accepted didn't exist for him. He saw everything in global terms and from God's perspective, refusing to accept sin. If the world was not evangelized, why not? If people were hungry, what could we do about it? Haggai didn't think like a Hindu—he refused to accept the world as it was. And I discovered that he was willing to accept personal responsibility to become an agent of change.

Toward the end of my month at the institute, John Haggai challenged me into the most painful introspection I have ever experienced. I know now it implanted a restlessness in me that would last for years, eventually causing me to leave India to search abroad for God's ultimate will in my life.

Haggai's challenge seemed simple at first. He wanted me to go to my room and write down—in one sentence—the single most important thing I was going to do with the rest of my life. He stipulated that it could not be self-centered or worldly in nature. And one more thing—it had to bring glory to God.

I went to my room to write that one sentence. But the paper remained blank for hours and days. Disturbed that I might not be reaching my full potential in Christ, I began at that conference to reevaluate every part of my lifestyle and ministry. I left the conference with the question still ringing in my ears, and for years I would continue to hear the words of John Haggai, "One thing . . . by God's grace you have to do one thing."

I left Singapore newly liberated to think of myself in terms of an individual for the first time. Up until that time—like most Asians—I always had viewed myself as part of a group, either my family or a Gospel team. Although I had no idea what special work God would have for me as an individual, I began thinking of doing my "personal best" for Him. The seeds for future change had been planted, and nothing could stop the approaching storms in my life.

While my greatest passion was still for the unreached villages of the North, I now was traveling all over India.

On one of these speaking trips in 1973, I was invited to teach at the spring Operation Mobilization training conference in Madras. That was where I first saw the attractive German girl. As a student in one of my classes, she impressed me with the simplicity of her faith. Soon I found myself thinking that if she were an Indian, she would be the kind of woman I would like to marry some day.

Once, when our eyes met, we held each other's gaze for a brief, extra moment, until I self-consciously broke the spell and quickly fled the room. I was uncomfortable in such male-female encounters. In our culture, single people seldom speak to each other. Even in church and on Gospel teams, the sexes are kept strictly separate.

Certain that I would never again see her, I pushed the thought of the attractive German girl from my mind. But marriage was on my mind. I had made a list of the six qualities I most wanted in a wife and frequently prayed for the right choice to be made for me.

Of course, in India, all marriages are arranged by the parents, and I would have to rely on their judgment in selecting the right person for my life partner. I wondered where my parents would find a wife who was willing to share my mobile lifestyle and commitment to the work of the Gospel. But as the conference ended, plans for the summer outreach soon crowded out these thoughts.

That summer, along with a few coworkers, I returned to all the places we had visited during the last few years in the state of Punjab. I had been in and out of the state many times and was eager to see the fruit of our evangelism there.

The breadbasket of India, with its population of 24 million, is dominated by turbaned Sikhs, a fiercely independent and hardworking people who have always been a caste of warriors.

Before the partition of India and Pakistan, the state also had a huge Muslim population. It remains one of the least evange lized and most neglected areas of the world.

We had trucked and street-preached our way through hundreds of towns and villages in this state over the previous two years. Although British missionaries had founded many hospitals and schools in the state, very few congregations of believers now existed. The intensely nationalistic Sikhs stubbornly refused to consider Christianity because they closely associated it with British colonialism.

I traveled with a good-sized team of men. A separate women's team also was assigned to the state, working out of Jullundur.

On my way north to link up with the men's team I would lead, I stopped in at the North India headquarters in New Delhi.

To my surprise, there she was again—the German girl. This time she was dressed in a sari, one of the most popular forms of our national dress. I learned she also had been assigned to work in Punjab for the summer with the women's team.

The local director asked me to escort her northward as far as Jullundur, and so we rode in the same van. I learned her name was Gisela, and the more I saw of her the more enchanted I became. She ate the food and drank the water and unconsciously followed all the rules of our culture. The little conversation we had focused on spiritual things and the lost villages of India. I soon realized I had finally found a soul mate who shared my vision and calling.

Romantic love, for most Indians, is something you read about only in storybooks. Daring cinema films, while they frequently deal with the concept, are careful to end the film in a proper Indian manner. So I was faced with the big problem of communicating my forbidden and impossible love. I said nothing to Gisela, of course. But something in her eyes told me we both understood. Could God be bringing us together?

In a few hours we would be separated again, and I reminded myself I had other things to do. Besides, I thought, at the end of the summer she'll be flying to Germany, and I'll probably never see her again. Throughout the summer, surprisingly, our paths did cross again. Each time I felt my love grow stronger. Then I tentatively took a chance at expressing my love with a letter.

Meanwhile, the Punjab survey broke my heart. In village after village, our literature and preaching appeared to have had little lasting impact. The fruit had not remained. Most of the villages we visited appeared just as illiterate, idolatrous and demon-controlled as ever. The people still were locked in disease, poverty and suffering. The Gospel, it seemed to me, hadn't taken root.

In one town I felt such deep despair I literally sat down on a curb and sobbed. I wept the bitter tears that only a child can cry.

"Your work is for nothing," taunted a demon in my ear. "Your words are rolling off these people like water off a duck's back!"

Without realizing I was burning out—or what was happening to me spiritually—I fell into listlessness. Like Jonah and Elijah, I was too tired to go on. I could see only one thing. The fruit of my work wasn't remaining. More than ever before, I needed time to reassess my ministry.

My coleaders, alarmed at my personal crisis and aware that something was deeply wrong, insisted I take a month off to recoup, so I went to Bombay.

While there, I corresponded with Gisela. She had, in the meantime, returned to Germany. I decided I would take two years off from the work to study and make some life choices about my ministry and possible marriage.

I began writing letters abroad and became interested in the possibility of attending a Bible school in England. I also had invitations to speak in churches in Germany. In December I bought an air ticket out of India planning to be in Europe for Christmas with Gisela's family.

While there I got the first tremors of what soon would become an earthquake-size case of culture shock. As the snow fell, it was obvious to everyone I soon would have to buy a winter coat and boots—obvious, that is, to everyone except me. One look at the price tags sent me into deep trauma. For the cost of my coat and boots in Germany, I could have lived comfortably for months back in India.

And this concept of living by faith was hard for Gisela's parents to accept. Here was this penniless street preacher from India, without a single dollar of his own, insisting he was going to school but he didn't know where and, by now, asking to marry their daughter.

One by one the miracles occurred, though, and God met every need.

First, a letter arrived from E.A. Gresham, a total stranger from Dallas, Texas, who was then regional director of the Fellowship of Christian Athletes. He had heard about me from a Scottish friend and invited me to come to the United States for two years of study at what was then the Criswell Bible Institute in Dallas. I replied positively and booked myself on a low-cost charter flight to New York with the last money I had.

This flight, it turned out, also was to become a miracle. Not knowing I needed a special student visa, I bought the ticket without the chance for refund. If I missed the flight, I would lose both my seat and the ticket.

Praying with my last ounce of faith, I asked God to intervene and somehow get the paperwork for the visa. As I prayed, a friend in Dallas, Texas, was strangely moved by God to get out of his car, go back to the office, and complete my paperwork and personally take it to the post office. In a continuous series of divinely arranged "coincidences," the forms arrived within hours of the deadline.

Before leaving for America, Gisela and I became engaged. I would go on to seminary alone, however. We had no idea when we would see each other again.

Four

I Walked in a Daze

As I changed planes for Dallas at JFK International in New York, I was overcome at the sights and sounds around me. Those of us who grow up in Europe and Asia hear stories about the affluence and prosperity of the United States, but until you see it with your own eyes, the stories seem like fairy tales.

Americans are more than just unaware of their affluence—they almost seem to despise it at times. Finding a lounge chair, I stared in amazement at how they treated their beautiful clothes and shoes. The richness of the fabrics and colors was beyond anything I had ever seen. As I would discover again and again, this nation routinely takes its astonishing wealth for granted.

As I would do many times—almost daily—in the weeks ahead, I compared their clothing to that of the native missionary evangelists whom I had left only a few weeks before. Many of them walk barefoot between villages or work in flimsy sandals. Their threadbare cotton garments would not be acceptable as cleaning rags in the United States. Then I discovered most Americans have closets full of clothing they wear only occasionally—and I remembered the years I traveled and worked with only the clothes on my back. And I had lived the normal lifestyle of most village evangelists.

Economist Robert Heilbroner describes the luxuries a typical American family would have to surrender if they lived among the 1 billion hungry people in the Two-Thirds World:

We begin by invading the house of our imaginary American family to strip it of its furniture. Everything goes: beds, chairs, tables, television sets, lamps. We will leave the family with a few old blankets, a kitchen table, a wooden chair. Along with the bureaus go the clothes. Each member of the family may keep in his wardrobe his oldest suit or dress, a shirt or blouse. We will permit a pair of shoes for the head of the family, but none for the wife or children.

We move to the kitchen. The appliances have already been taken out, so we turn to the cupboards. . . . The box of matches may stay, a small bag of flour, some sugar and salt. A few moldy potatoes, already in the garbage can, must be rescued, for they will provide much of tonight's meal. We will leave a handful of onions and a dish of dried beans. All the rest we take away: the meat, the fresh vegetables, the canned goods, the crackers, the candy.

Now we have stripped the house: the bathroom has been dismantled, the running water shut off, the electric wires taken out. Next we take away the house. The family can move to the tool shed. . . . Communications must go next. No more newspapers, magazines, books—not that they are missed, since we must take away our family's literacy as well. Instead, in our shantytown we will allow one radio. . . .

Now government services must go next. No more postmen, no more firemen. There is a school, but it is three miles away and consists of two classrooms. . . . There are, of course, no hospitals or doctors nearby. The nearest clinic is ten miles away and is tended by a midwife. It can be reached by bicycle, provided the family has a bicycle, which is unlikely. . . .

Finally, money. We will allow our family a cash hoard of five dollars. This will prevent our breadwinner from experiencing the tragedy of an Iranian peasant who went blind because he could not raise the $3.94 which he mistakenly thought he needed to receive admission to a hospital where he could have been cured.[1]

This is an accurate description of the lifestyle and world from which I came. From the moment I touched foot on American soil, I walked in an unbelieving daze. How can two so different economies coexist simultaneously on the earth? Everything was so overpowering and confusing to me at first. Not only did I have to learn the simplest procedures like using the pay telephones and making change—but as a sensitive Christian, I found myself constantly making spiritual evaluations of everything I saw.

As the days passed into weeks, I began with alarm to understand how misplaced are the spiritual values of most Western believers. Sad to say, it appeared to me that for the most part they had absorbed the same humanistic and materialistic values that dominated the secular culture. Almost immediately I sensed an awesome judgment was hanging over the United States—and that I had to warn God's people that He was not going to lavish this abundance on them forever. But the message was still not formed in my heart, and it would be many years before I would feel the anointing and courage to speak out against such sin.

Meanwhile, in Texas, a land that in many ways epitomizes America, I reeled with shock at the most common things. My hosts eagerly pointed out what they considered their greatest achievements. I nodded with politeness as they showed me their huge churches, high-rise buildings and universities. But these didn't impress me very much. After all, I had seen the Golden Temple in Amritsar, the Taj Mahal, the Palaces of Jhans, the University of Baroda in Gujarat.

What impresses visitors from the Two-Thirds World are the simple things Americans take for granted: fresh water available 24 hours a day, unlimited electrical power, telephones that work and a most remarkable network of paved roads. Compared to Western countries, things in Asia are still in the process of development. At the time, we still had no television in India, but my American hosts seemed to have TV sets in every room—and they operated day and night. This ever-present blast of media disturbed me. For some reason, Americans seemed to have a need to surround themselves with noise all the time. Even in their cars, I noticed the radios were on even when no one was listening.

Why do they always have to be either entertained or entertaining? I wondered. It was as if they were trying to escape from a guilt they had not yet defined or even identified.

I was constantly aware of how large—and overweight—most Americans seemed to be. Americans need big cars, big homes and large furniture, because they are big people.

I was amazed at how important eating, drinking, smoking and even drug use were in the Western lifestyle. Even among Christians, food was a major part of fellowship events.

This, of course, is not bad in itself. "Love feasts" were an important part of the New Testament church life. But eating can be taken to extremes. One of the ironies of this is the relatively small price North Americans pay for food. In 1998, personal expenditures in the United States averaged $19,049 per person, of which $1,276 (6.7 percent) went for food, leaving a comfortable $17,773 for other expenses. In India, the average person had only $276 to spend, of which $134 (48.4 percent) went for food, leaving a scant $142 for other needs for the entire year.[2] I had lived with this reality every day, but Americans have real trouble thinking in these terms.

Often when I spoke at a church, the people would appear moved as I told of the suffering and needs of the native evangelists. They usually took an offering and presented me with a check for what seemed like a great amount of money. Then with their usual hospitality, they invited me to eat with the leaders following the meeting. To my horror, the food and "fellowship" frequently cost more than the money they had just given to missions. And I was amazed to find that American families routinely eat enough meat at one meal to feed an Asian family for a week. No one ever seemed to notice this but me, and slowly I realized they just had not heard the meaning of my message. They were simply incapable of understanding the enormous needs overseas.

Even today I sometimes cannot freely order food when traveling in the United States. I look at the costs and realize how far the same amount of money will go in India, Myanmar (formerly Burma) or the Philippines. Suddenly I am not quite as hungry as I was before.

Many native missionaries and their families experience days without food—not because they are fasting voluntarily but because they have no money to buy rice. This occurs especially when they start new work in villages where there are no Christians.

Remembering the heartbreaking suffering of the native brethren, I sometimes refused to eat the desserts so often served to me. I am sure this made no difference in supplying food to hungry families, but I couldn't bear to take pleasure in eating while Christian workers in Asia were going hungry. The need became real to me through the ministry of Brother Moses Paulose, who is today one of the native missionaries we sponsor.

Millions of poor, uneducated fisher-folk live along the thousands of islands and endless miles of coastal backwaters in Asia. Their homes usually are small huts made of leaves, and their lifestyles are simple—hard work and little pleasure. These fishermen and their families are some of the most unreached people in the world. But God called Paulose and his family to take the Gospel to the unreached fishing villages of Tamil Nadu on the east coast of India.

I remember visiting Paulose's family. One of the first things he discovered when he began visiting the villages was that the literacy rate was so low he could not use tracts or printed materials effectively. He decided to use slides, but had no projector or money to purchase one. So he made repeated trips to a hospital where he sold his blood until he had the money he needed.

It was exciting to see the crowds his slide projector attracted. As soon as he began to put up the white sheet that served as a screen, thousands of adults and children gathered along the beach. Mrs. Paulose sang Gospel songs over a loudspeaker powered by a car battery, and their five-year-old son quoted Bible verses to passersby.

When the sun had set, Brother Paulose began his slide presentation. For several hours, thousands sat in the sand, listening to the Gospel message while the sea murmured in the background. When we finally packed to leave, I had to walk carefully to avoid stepping on the hundreds of children sleeping on the sand.

But the tragedy behind all this was the secret starvation Paulose and his family faced. Once I heard his long-suffering wife comforting the children and urging them to drink water from a baby bottle in order to hold off the pangs of hunger. There was not enough money in the house for milk. Ashamed to let the non-Christian neighbors know he was without food, Paulose kept the windows and doors in his one-room rented house closed so they could not hear the cries of his four hungry children.

On another occasion, one of his malnourished children fell asleep in school because he was so weak from hunger. "I am ashamed to tell the teacher or our neighbors," he told me. "Only God, our children, and my wife and I know the real story. We have no complaints or even unhappiness. We're joyfully and totally content in our service of the Lord. It is a privilege to be counted worthy to suffer for His sake. . . ."

Even when the teacher punished his children for lack of attention in class, Paulose would not tell his secret suffering and bring shame on the name of Christ. Fortunately, in this case, we were able to send immediate support to him, thanks to the help of generous American Christians. But for too many others, the story does not end as happily.

Is it God's fault that men like Brother Paulose are going hungry? I do not think so. God has provided more than enough money to meet Paulose's needs and all the needs of the Two-Thirds World. The needed money is in the highly developed nations of the West. North American Christians alone, without much sacrifice, can meet all the needs of the churches in the Two-Thirds World.

A friend in Dallas recently pointed out a new church building that cost $74 million. While this thought was still exploding in my mind, he pointed out another $7 million church building going up less than a minute away.

These extravagant buildings are insanity from a Two-Thirds World perspective. The $74 million spent on one new building in the United States could build more than 7,000 average-sized churches in India. The same $74 million would be enough to guarantee the evangelization of a whole state—or even some of the smaller countries of Asia.

But I rarely spoke out on these subjects. I realized I was a guest. The Americans who had built these buildings had also built the school I was now attending, and they were paying my tuition to attend. It amazed me, though, that these buildings had been constructed to worship Jesus, who said, "The foxes have holes, and the birds of the air have nests; but the Son of man hath not where to lay his head" (Matthew 8:20).

In Asia today, Christ is still wandering homeless. He is looking for a place to lay His head, but in temples "not made with human hands." Until they can build a facility of their own, our newborn Christians usually meet in their homes. In non-Christian communities, it is often impossible to rent church facilities.

There is such an emphasis on church buildings in the United States that we sometimes forget that the Church is the people— not the place where the people meet.

But God has not called me to fight against church building programs. I think what troubles me much more than the waste is that these efforts represent a worldly mindset. Why can't we at least earmark 10 percent of our Christian giving for the cause of world evangelism? If Christians in the United States alone had made this commitment in 2000, there would have been nearly $10 billion available for Gospel outreach![3]

And what is more, if we had used these funds to support native missions, we could have fielded an army of evangelists the size of a major city.

Five

A Nation Asleep in Bondage

Religion, I discovered, is a multi-billion dollar business in the United States. Entering churches, I was astonished at the carpeting, furnishings, air-conditioning and ornamentation. Many churches have gymnasiums and fellowships that cater to a busy schedule of activities having little or nothing to do with Christ. The orchestras, choirs, "special" music—and sometimes even the preaching—seemed to me more like entertainment than worship.

Many North American Christians live isolated from reality—not only from the needs of the poor overseas, but even from the poor in their own cities. Amidst all the affluence live millions of terribly poor people left behind as Christians have moved into the suburbs. I found that believers are ready to get involved in almost any activity that looks spiritual but allows them to escape their responsibility to the Gospel.

One morning, for example, I picked up a popular Christian magazine containing many interesting articles, stories and reports from all over the world—most written by famous Christian leaders in the West. I noticed that this magazine offered ads for 21 Christian colleges, seminaries and correspondence courses; five different English translations of the Bible; seven conferences and retreats; five new Christian films; 19 commentaries and devotional books; seven Christian health or diet programs; and five fund-raising services.

But that was not all. There were ads for all kinds of products and services: counseling, chaplaincy services, writing courses, church steeples, choir robes, wall crosses, baptisteries and water heaters, T-shirts, records, tapes, adoption agencies, tracts, poems, gifts, book clubs and pen pals. It was all rather impressive. Probably none of these things was wrong in itself, but it bothered me that one nation should have such spiritual luxury while 40,000 people were dying in my homeland every day without hearing the Gospel even once.

If the affluence of America impressed me, the affluence of Christians impressed me even more. The United States has about 5,000 Christian book and gift stores,[1] carrying varieties of products beyond my ability to imagine—and many secular stores also carry religious books. All this while 6,800 of the world's 13,500 languages are still without a single portion of the Bible published in their own language![2] In his book *My Billion Bible Dream*, Rochunga Pudaite says, "Eighty-five percent of all Bibles printed today are in English for the nine percent of the world who read English. Eighty percent of the world's people have never owned a Bible while Americans have an average of four in every household."[3]

Besides books, 8,000 Christian magazines and newspapers flourish.[4] More than 1,600 Christian radio stations broadcast the Gospel full-time,[5] while many countries don't even have their first Christian radio station. A tiny 0.1 percent of all Christian radio and television programming is directed toward the unevangelized world.[6]

The saddest observation I can make about most of the religious communication activity of the Western world is this: Little, if any, of this media is designed to reach unbelievers. Almost all is entertainment for the saints.

The United States, with its 600,000 congregations or groups, is blessed with 1.5 million full-time Christian workers, or one full-time religious leader for every 182 people in the nation.[7] What a difference this is from the rest of the world, where more than 2 billion people are still unreached with the Gospel. The unreached or "hidden peoples" have only one missionary working for every 78,000 people,[8] and there are still 1,240 distinct cultural groups in the world without a single church among them to preach the Gospel.[9] These are the masses for whom Christ wept and died.

One of the most impressive blessings in America is religious liberty. Not only do Christians have access to radio and television, unheard of in most nations of Asia, but they are also free to hold meetings, evangelize and print literature. How different this is from many Asian nations in which government persecution of Christians is common and often legal.

Such was the case in Nepal, where until recently it was illegal to change one's religion or to influence others to change their religion. Christians often faced prison there for their faith.

One native missionary there served time in 14 different prisons between 1960 and 1975. He spent 10 out of those 15 years suffering torture and ridicule for preaching the Gospel to his people.

His ordeal began when he baptized nine new believers and was arrested for doing so. The new converts, five men and four women, also were arrested, and each was sentenced to a year in prison. He was sentenced to serve six years for influencing them.

Nepali prisons are typically Asian—literally dungeons of death. About 25 to 30 people are jammed into one small room with no ventilation or sanitation. The smell is so bad that newcomers often pass out in less than half an hour.

The place where Brother P. and his fellow believers were sent was crawling with lice and cockroaches. Prisoners slept on dirt floors. Rats and mice gnawed on fingers and toes during the night. In the winter there was no heat; in summer no ventilation. For food, the prisoners were allowed one cup of rice each day, but they had to build a fire on the ground to cook it. The room was constantly filled with smoke because there was no chimney. On that inadequate diet, most prisoners became seriously ill, and the stench of vomit was added to the other putrefying odors. Yet miraculously, none of the Christians was sick for even one day during the entire year.

After serving their one-year sentences, the nine new believers were released. Then the authorities decided to break Brother P. They took his Bible away from him, chained him hand and foot, then forced him through a low doorway into a tiny cubicle previously used to store bodies of dead prisoners until relatives came to claim them.

In the damp darkness, the jailer predicted his sanity would not last more than a few days. The room was so small that Brother P. could not stand up or even stretch out on the floor. He could not build a fire to cook, so other prisoners slipped food under the door to keep him alive.

Lice ate away his underwear, but he could not scratch because of the chains, which soon cut his wrists and ankles to the bone. It was winter, and he nearly froze to death several times. He could not tell day from night, but as he closed his eyes, God let him see the pages of the New Testament. Although his Bible had been taken away, he was still able to read it in total darkness. It sustained him as he endured the terrible torture. For three months he was not allowed to speak to another human being.

Brother P. was transferred to many other prisons. In each, he continually shared his faith with both guards and prisoners.

Although Brother P. continues to move in and out of prisons, he has refused to form secret churches. "How can a Christian keep silent?" he asks. "How can a church go underground? Jesus died openly for us. He did not try to hide on the way to the cross. We also must speak out boldly for Him regardless of the consequences."

Coming from India, where I was beaten and stoned for my faith, I know what it is to be a persecuted minority in my own country. When I set foot on Western soil, I could sense a spirit of religious liberty. Americans have never known the fear of persecution. Nothing seems impossible to them.

From India, I always had looked to the United States as a fortress of Christianity. With the abundance of both spiritual and material things, affluence unsurpassed by any nation on earth, and a totally unfettered church, I expected to see a bold witness. God's grace obviously has been poured out on this nation and Church in a way no other people ever have experienced.

Instead I found a Church in spiritual decline. American believers were still the leading givers to missions, but this appeared due more to historical accident than the deep-set conviction I expected to find. As I spoke in churches and met average Christians, I discovered they had terrible misconceptions about the missionary mandate of the Church. In church meetings, as I listened to the questions of my hosts and heard their comments about the Two-Thirds World, my heart would almost burst with pain. These people, I knew, were capable of so much more. They were dying spiritually, but I knew God wanted to give them life again. He wanted His Church to recover its moral mandate and sense of mission.

I didn't yet know how. I didn't know when. But I knew one thing: God did not shower such great blessing on this nation for the Christians to live in extravagance, in self-indulgence and in spiritual weakness.

By faith, I could see a revival coming—the Body of Christ rediscovering the power of the Gospel and their obligation to it. But for the time being, all I could do was sense how wrong the situation was—and pray. God had not given me the words to articulate what I was seeing—or a platform from which to speak. Instead He still had some important lessons to teach me, and I was to learn them in this alien land far from my beloved India.

Six

What Are You Doing Here?

The Bible says that "some plant" and "others water." The living God now took me halfway around the world to teach me about watering. Before He could trust me again with the planting, I had to learn the lesson I had been avoiding in India—the importance of the local church in God's master plan for world evangelism.

It really started through one of those strange coincidences —a divine appointment that only a sovereign God could engineer. By now I was a busy divinity student in Dallas at the Criswell Bible Institute, intently soaking up every one of my classes. Thanks to the scholarship God had so miraculously provided, I was able to dig into God's Word as never before. For the first time I was doing formal, in-depth study, and the Bible was revealing many of its secrets to me.

After my first term, Gisela and I were married, and she joined me in Dallas at the beginning of the next school term, October 1974. Except for preaching engagements and opportunities to share about Asia on weekends, I was fully absorbed in my studies and establishing our new home.

One weekend a fellow student invited me to fill the pulpit at a little church he was pastoring in Dallas. Although it was an American congregation, there were many Native Americans in fellowship.

Gisela was especially thrilled because through much of her childhood she had prayed to be a missionary to "Red Indians on the Great Plains of America." While other schoolgirls dreamed of marriage and a Prince Charming, she was praying about doing ministry work among Native Americans. Much to my surprise, I found she had collected and read more than 100 books about the tribal life and history of Native Americans.

Strangely challenged and burdened for this little congregation, I preached my heart out. Never once did I mention my vision and burden for Asia. Instead I expounded Scripture verse by verse. A great love welled up in me for these people.

Although I did not know it, my pastor friend turned in his resignation the same day. The deacons invited me to come back the next week and the next. God gave us a supernatural love for these people, and they loved us back. Late that month the church board invited me to become the pastor, at the age of 23. When Gisela and I accepted the call, I instantly found myself carrying a burden for these people 24 hours a day.

More than once, I shamefacedly remembered how I had despised pastors and their problems back in India. Now that I was patching up relationships, healing wounded spirits and holding a group together, I started to see things in a wholly different light. Some of the problems God's people face are the same worldwide, so I preached against sin and for holy living. Other problems (such as divorce, an epidemic in the West but almost unheard of in India when I first came to this country) I was completely unprepared to handle.

Although my weight had increased to 106 pounds, I still nearly collapsed when I attempted to baptize a 250-pound convert at one of our regular water baptisms. People came to Christ continually, making ours a growing, soul-winning church with a hectic round of meetings that went six nights a week.

The days passed quickly into months. When I wasn't in

classes, I was with my people giving myself to them with the same abandonment that characterized my village preaching in North India. We learned to visit in homes, call on the sick in hospitals, marry and bury. Gisela and I were involved in the lives of our people day and night. Because we had several Native American tribal groups represented in the congregation, as well as "anglos," we soon found we were ministering to several different cultures simultaneously.

The "staying power" and disciple-making were what my ministry in North India had lacked. I saw why I had failed in Punjab. Holding evangelistic crusades and bringing people to Christ are not enough: Someone has to stay behind and nurture the new believers into maturity.

For the first time I began to understand the goal of all mission work: the "perfecting" of the saints into sanctified, committed disciples of Christ. Jesus commanded us to go to all the nations, baptizing them and teaching them to obey all the things He had revealed. The Gospel-team ministry I had led in India was going, but we weren't staying to do the teaching.

The church—a group of believers—is God's ordained place for the discipleship process to take place. God's Plan A for the redemption of the world is the Church, and He has no Plan B.

As I shepherded a local congregation, the Lord revealed to me that the same qualities are needed in native missionary evangelists, the men and women who could reach the hidden peoples of Asia. In my imagination I saw these same discipleship concepts being implanted in India and throughout Asia. Like the early Methodist circuit riders who planted churches on the American frontier, I could see our evangelists adding church planting to their evangelistic efforts.

But even as the concept captured me, I realized it would take an army of people—an army of God—to accomplish this task.

In India alone, 500,000 villages are without a Gospel witness. And then there are China, Southeast Asia and the islands. We would need a million workers to finish the task.

This idea was too big for me to accept, so I pushed it from my mind. After all, I reasoned, God had called me to this little church here in Dallas, and He was blessing my ministry. I was getting very comfortable where I was. The church supported us well; and with our first baby on the way, I had begun to accept the Western way of life as my own, complete with a house, automobile, credit cards, insurance policies and bank accounts.

My formal schooling continued as I prepared to settle into building up the church. But my peace about staying in Dallas was slipping away. By the end of 1976 and early in 1977, I heard an accusing voice every time I stood in the pulpit: "What are you doing here? While you preach to an affluent American congregation, millions are going to hell in Asia. Have you forgotten your people?"

A terrible inner conflict developed. I was unable to recognize the voice. Was it God? Was it my own conscience? Was it demonic? In desperation, I decided to wait upon God for His plan. I had said we would go anywhere, do anything. But we had to hear definitely from God. I could not go on working with that tormenting voice. I announced to the church that I was praying, and I asked them to join with me in seeking the will of God for our future ministry.

"I seem to have no peace," I admitted to them, "about either staying in the United States or returning to India."

I wondered, "What is God really trying to say to me?" As I prayed and fasted, God revealed Himself to me in a vision. It came back several times before I understood the revelation. Many faces would appear before me—the faces of Asian men and their families from many lands. They were holy men and women, with looks of dedication on their faces. Gradually, I understood these people to be an image of the army of God that is now being raised up to take the Gospel to every part of Asia.

Then the Lord spoke to me: "They cannot speak what you will speak. They will not go where you will go. You are called to be their servant. You must go where I will send you on their behalf. You are called to be their servant."

As lightning floods the sky in a storm, my whole life passed before me in that instant. I had never spoken English until I was 16, yet now I was ministering in this strange language. I had never worn shoes before I was 17. I was born and raised in a jungle village. Suddenly I realized I had nothing to be proud of; my talents or skills had not brought me to America. My coming here was an act of God's sovereign will. He wanted me to cross cultures, to marry a German wife and live in an alien land to give me the experiences I would need to serve in a new missionary movement.

"I have led you to this point," said God. "Your lifetime call is to be the servant of the unknown brethren—men whom I have called out and scattered among the villages of Asia." Knowing that at last I had found my life's work, I eagerly rushed to share my new vision with my church leaders and executives of missionary societies. To my utter bewilderment, God seemed to have forgotten to tell anyone but me.

My friends thought I was crazy. Mission leaders questioned either my integrity or my qualifications—and sometimes both. Church leaders whom I trusted and respected wrapped fatherly arms around my shoulders and counseled me against undue emotionalism. Suddenly, through a simple announcement, I found myself alone—under attack and forced to defend myself. I knew that had I not waited for such a clear calling, I would have collapsed under those early storms of unbelief and doubt. But I remained convinced of my call—certain that God was initiating a new day in world missions. Still, no one seemed to catch my enthusiasm.

Secretly I had prided myself on being a good speaker and salesman, but nothing I could do or say seemed to turn the tide of public opinion. While I was arguing that "new wine needed new wineskins," others could only ask, "Where is the new wine?"

My only comfort was Gisela, who had been with me in India and accepted the vision without question. In moments of discouragement, when even my faith wavered, she refused to allow us to let go of the vision. Rebuffed but certain we had heard God correctly, we planted the first seeds by ourselves.

I wrote to an old friend in India whom I had known and trusted for years, asking him to help me select some needy native missionaries who already were doing outstanding work. I promised to come and meet them later, and we started planning a survey trip to seek out more qualified workers.

Slowly, a portion of our own personal income and resources were sent as missionary support to India. I became compulsive. Soon I could not buy a hamburger or drink a cola without feeling guilty. Realizing we had fallen into the trap of materialism, we quietly sold everything we could, pulled our savings out of the bank and cashed in my life insurance. I remembered how one of my seminary professors solemnly instructed his class of young "preacher boys" to lay aside money every month for emergencies, purchase life insurance and build equity in a home.

But I could not find any of this in the New Testament commands of Christ. Why was it necessary to save our money in bank accounts when Jesus commanded us not to lay up treasures on this earth? "Haven't I commanded you to live by faith?" asked the Holy Spirit.

So Gisela and I conformed our lives literally to the New Testament commands of Christ regarding money and material

LEFT: **K.P.'S MOTHER** faithfully prayed and fasted every Friday for three and a half years, asking God to call one of her sons to be a missionary. Her prayer was answered when K.P. began to serve the Lord at the age of 16.

BELOW: **K.P. YOHANNAN** (fifth from left) with an Operation Mobilization evangelism team in 1971. Next to him is Greg Livingstone, international director of Frontiers.

MILLIONS OF SOULS in many Asian nations worship countless gods and goddesses. Deeply religious and sincere, they offer all they have to these deities, hoping to find forgiveness of sin.

GOSPEL FOR ASIA'S U.S. HOME TEAM STAFF—2003. These dedicated brothers and sisters serve as a vital link between thousands of Christians here in the West and an army of Asian missionaries on the front lines. Similar home team staffs serve with GFA in Canada, Germany, the United Kingdom and New Zealand.

THIS TRIBAL WOMAN represents many unreached people groups who have never heard Jesus' name. Located in the heart of the 10/40 Window, India has the largest number of unreached people groups in the world today.

ABOVE: **K.P. AND HIS WIFE, GISELA,** were both 23 when the Lord brought them together to serve Him with one purpose and one goal—to live for Him and to give all they had to reach the lost world. That was in 1974. Today they joyfully continue on—that this generation may come to know the Lord Jesus Christ.

LEFT: **THEIR CHILDREN, DANIEL AND SARAH,** prayed from an early age that the Lord would call them to be missionaries. After finishing high school, they went on to study at Gospel for Asia's seminary and now serve the Lord on the mission field.

possessions. I even traded in my late model car for a cheaper used one. The difference went straight to India. It was a joy to make these little sacrifices for the native brethren. Besides, I knew that it was the only way we could get the mission started.

Please understand. It is not necessarily wrong to have life insurance or a savings account. This was the way the Lord was leading my family. How the Lord leads you may be different. This is what is important—each one of us is responsible for how we obey what He has said and follow Him alone.

In those early days, what kept me going was the assurance that there was no other way. Even if people did not understand that we had to start a native missionary movement, I felt an obligation to the knowledge of God's call. I knew Western missions alone could not get the job done. Because my own nation and many others were closed to outsiders, we had to turn to the native believers. Even if Western missionaries somehow were permitted back, the cost of sending them would be in the billions each year. Native evangelists could do the same for only a fraction of the cost.

I never told anyone that I eventually would need such huge sums of money. They already thought I was crazy for wanting to support 8 or 10 missionaries a month out of my own income. What would they think if I said I needed millions of dollars a year to field an army of God? But I knew it was possible. Several Western missionary societies and charities already were dealing with annual budgets that size. I saw no reason why we couldn't do the same.

But as logical as it all was in my mind, I had some bitter lessons to learn. Giving birth to a new mission society was going to take much more energy and start-up capital than I ever could imagine. I had a lot to learn about the United States and the way things are done here. But I knew nothing about that yet. I just knew it had to be done.

With youthful zest, Gisela and I went to India to do our first field survey. We returned a month later, penniless but committed to organizing what eventually would become Gospel for Asia.

Soon after our return, I revealed my decision to the congregation. Reluctantly we cut the cords of fellowship and made plans to move to Eufaula, Oklahoma, where another pastor friend had offered me some free space to open offices for the mission.

On the last day at the church, I tearfully preached my farewell sermon. When the last goodbye was said and the last hand was grasped, I locked the door and paused on the steps. I felt the hand of God lifting the mantle from my shoulders. God was releasing me of the burden for this church and the people of this place. As I strolled across the gravel driveway, the final mystery of Christian service became real to me.

Pastors—like missionary evangelists—are placed in the harvest fields of this world by God. No mission society, denomination, bishop, pope or superintendent calls a person to such service. In Gospel for Asia, I would not presume to ordain and call the native brethren but simply be a servant to the ones whom God already had chosen for His service.

Once settled in Oklahoma, I sought counsel from older Christian leaders, listening eagerly to anyone who would give me advice. Everywhere I went, I asked questions. I knew God had called me, and much of the advice I got was suicidal and destructive. I found we had to learn most of our lessons by painful trial and error. The only way I escaped several disastrous decisions was my stubborn refusal to compromise the vision God had given. If something fit in with what God had said to me, then I considered it. If not—no matter how attractive it appeared—I refused. The secret of following God's will, I discovered, usually is wrapped up in rejecting the good for God's best.

One piece of advice did stick, however. Every Christian leader should have this engraved in his subconscious: No matter what you do, never take yourself too seriously. Paul Smith, founder of Bible Translations on Tape, was the first executive to say that to me, and I think it is one of the best single fragments of wisdom I have received from anyone.

God always chooses the foolish things of this world to confound the wise. He shows His might only on the behalf of those who trust in Him. Humility is the place where all Christian service begins.

Seven

"It Is a Privilege"

We began Gospel for Asia without any kind of plan for regular involvement, but God soon gave us one. On one of my first trips, I went to Wheaton, Illinois, where I called on almost all the evangelical mission leaders. A few encouraged me—but not one offered the money we then needed desperately to keep going another day. The friend I stayed with, however, suggested we start a sponsorship plan through which North American families and individuals could support a native missionary regularly. It turned out to be just what we needed.

The idea—to lay aside one dollar a day for a native evangelist—gave us an instant handle for a program anyone could understand. I asked everyone I met if he or she would help sponsor a native missionary for one dollar a day. Some said yes, and that is how the mission began to get regular donors.

Today, this pledge plan is still the heart of our fund-raising efforts. We send the money—100 percent of it—to the field, sponsoring thousands of missionaries each month in this way.

Because I was sending all the pledge money overseas, we still were faced with the need to cover our overhead and living expenses here in the United States. Time and time again—just when we were at our lowest point—God miraculously intervened to keep us and the ministry going.

One Sunday when we were down to our last dollar, I drove our old $125 Nova to a nearby church for worship. I knew no one and sat in the last row. When it came time to take the offering, I quickly made an excuse to God and held on to that last dollar.

"This is my last dollar," I prayed desperately, "and I need to buy gas to get back home." But knowing God loves a cheerful giver, I stopped fighting and sacrificed that last dollar to the Lord.

As I left the church, an old man came up to me. I had never seen him before and never have since. He shook my hand silently, and I could feel a folded piece of paper in his palm. I knew instinctively that it was money. In the car, I opened my hand to find a neatly folded $10 bill.

Another afternoon, I sat grimly sulking on our sofa in Eufaula. Gisela was busy in the kitchen, avoiding my eyes. She said nothing, but both of us knew there wasn't any food in the house.

"So," said a coy voice from the enemy, "this is how you and your God provide for the family, eh?" Up until that moment, I don't think I had ever felt such helplessness. Here we were, in the middle of Oklahoma. Even if I had wanted to ask someone for help, I didn't know where to turn. Things had gotten so low I had offered to get a job, but Gisela was the one who refused. She was terrified that I would get into the world of business and not have time to work for the native brethren. For her there was no choice. It was to wait on the Lord. He would provide.

As the demonic voice continued to taunt me, I just sat still under the abuse. I had used up my last bit of faith, declaring a positive confession and praising God. Now I sat numb.

A knock came at the door. Gisela went to answer it. I was in no mood to meet anyone. Someone brought two boxes of groceries to our doorstep. These friends had no way of knowing our need—but we knew the source was God.

During those days, our needs continued to be met on a day-to-day basis, and I never had to borrow from the missionary support funds. I am convinced now that God knew the many trials ahead and wanted to teach us to have faith and trust in Him alone—even when I could not see Him.

In some way, which I still do not really understand, the trying of our faith works patience and hope into the fabric of our Christian lives. No one, I am convinced, will follow Jesus very long without tribulation. It is His way of demonstrating His presence. Sufferings and trials—like persecution—are a normal part of the Christian walk. We must learn to accept them joyfully if we are to grow through them, and I think this is true for ministries as well as individuals. Gospel for Asia was having its first wilderness experience, and the Oklahoma days were characterized by periods of the most painful waiting I had ever faced. We were alone in a strange land, utterly at the end of our own strength and desperately dependent on God.

Speaking engagements were hard to come by in the early days, but they were the only way we could grow. Nobody knew my name or the name of Gospel for Asia. I still was having a hard time explaining what we were all about. I knew our mission in my heart, but I hadn't learned to articulate it yet for outsiders. In a few short months, I had used up all the contacts I had.

Setting up a speaking tour took weeks of waiting, writing and calling. By the winter of 1980, I was ready to start my first major tour. I bought a budget air ticket that gave me unlimited travel for 21 days—and somehow I managed to make appointments in 18 cities. My itinerary would take me through the Southwest, from Dallas to Los Angeles.

On the day of my departure, a terrible winter storm hit the region. All the buses—including the one I planned to take from Eufaula, Oklahoma, to Dallas—were cancelled.

Our old Nova had some engine problems, so a neighbor

offered to let me use an old pickup truck without a heater. The vehicle looked as if it could not make it to the next town, let alone the six-hour drive to Dallas. But it was either the pickup or nothing. If I missed my flight, the tightly packed schedule would be ruined. I had to go now.

Doing the best I could to stay warm, I put on two pairs of socks and all the clothing I could. But even with the extra protection, I was on U.S. Highway 75 only a few minutes when it appeared I had made a terrible mistake. A freezing snow covered the windshield within minutes. After every mile I had to stop, get out and scrape the windows again. Soon my feet and gloves were soaked and frozen. I realized that the journey was going to take a lot longer than the six hours I had left. In my worst scenario, I saw the newspaper headlines reading "Preacher Freezes to Death in Winter Storm." My head dropped to the steering wheel, and I cried out to God.

"Lord, if You want me to go—if You believe in this mission and in my helping the native evangelists—please do something."

As I looked up, I saw a miracle on the windshield. The ice was melting rapidly before my eyes. Warmth flooded the truck. I looked at the heater, but nothing was coming out. Outside, the storm continued to rage. It kept up all the way to Dallas, but the truck was always warm, and the windshield was always clear.

This miraculous start was only the beginning of blessings. For the next 18 days, I gained new sponsors and donors in every city. The Lord gave me favor in the eyes of all I met.

On the last day of the tour, a man in California came to the pastor and said that God had told him to donate his second car to me. I cancelled my airline reservation and drove all the way home, rejoicing in the car God had provided. I received new inspiration and instruction from God as I drove.

I followed this pattern for the next few years, surviving from one meeting to the next, living out of the trunk of the car and speaking anywhere I could get an invitation. All our new donors and sponsors came from one-on-one contacts and through the meetings. I knew there were faster, more efficient ways to acquire new donors. Many times I studied the mass mailings and radio/TV broadcasts of other missions, but everything they were doing required large sums of money, which I did not have and did not know how to get.

Eventually, we moved back to Dallas. By now I was traveling full-time for the ministry, and the strain was taking a heavy toll both on my family and on me. I was starting to burn out—and I almost hated the work.

Two factors were wearing me down.

First, I felt like a beggar. It is hard on the flesh to be traveling and asking for money day after day and night after night. It was almost becoming a sales operation for me, and I stopped feeling good about myself.

Second, I was discouraged by the poor response—especially from churches and pastors. Many times it seemed as if my presence threatened them. Where, I wondered, was the fraternal fellowship of working together in the extension of the kingdom? Many days I called on people for hours to get only one or two new sponsors. Pastors and mission committees listened to me and promised to call back, but I never heard from them again. It always seemed as though I was competing against the building fund, new carpets for the fellowship hall or next Saturday night's Jesus rock concert.

Despite the solemn message of death, suffering and need I was presenting, people still left the meetings with laughter and gossip on their lips. I was offended at the spirit of jocularity in the churches: It wounded me. So many times we went out to eat after I had just shared the tragedy of the thousands who starve to death daily or the millions of homeless people living on the streets of Asia. Because of this, I was becoming angry and judgmental. As I felt uglier and uglier inside, depression settled in.

Early in 1981—while driving alone between meetings in a borrowed car near Greensboro, North Carolina—all the dark feelings of psychological burn-out crept over me. I had a full-fledged pity party, feeling sorry for myself and the hard life I was leading.

With a start, I began to tremble with fear. Suddenly I felt the presence of someone else. I realized that the Spirit of the Lord was speaking.

"I am not in any trouble," He chided, "that I need someone to beg for Me or help Me out. I made no promises that I will not keep. It is not the largeness of the work that matters, but only doing what I command. All I ask of you is that you be a servant. For all who join with you in the work, it will be a privilege—a light burden for them."

The words echoed in my mind. This is His work, I told myself. Why am I making it mine? The burden is light. Why am I making it heavy? The work is a privilege. Why am I making it a chore?

I instantly repented of my sinful attitudes. God was sharing His work with me, and He was speaking of others who would join me. Although I still was doing the work alone, it was exciting to think others would be joining with me and that they too would find the burden to be light. From that moment until this, I have not been overpowered by the burden of heading Gospel for Asia. I find building this mission an exciting, joyful job. Even my preaching has changed. My posture is different. Today the pressure is gone. No more do I feel I have to beg audiences or make them feel guilty.

Because the work of Gospel for Asia—and the whole native missionary movement—is initiated by God, it does not need the worries and guidance of man. Whether our goal is to support 10,000 or 10 million missionaries, whether it is working in 10 states or 100, or whether I must supervise a staff of 5 or 500, I still can approach this work without stress. For this is His work, and our burden is easy.

By now we had rented offices in Dallas, and the mission was growing steadily. I sensed it was time for a big step forward, and waited upon God for a miracle breakthrough. We had hundreds of native missionaries waiting for support by mid-1981, and I realized that we soon would have thousands more. I no longer could communicate personally with every new sponsor. I knew we had to use mass media. But I didn't know where to begin.

Then I met Brother Lester Roloff.

Brother Roloff is now with the Lord, but during his life he was a rugged individualist who preached his way across five decades of outstanding Christian service. Near the end of his life, I approached him for help in our ministry. His staff person, in arranging the interview, said I would have only five minutes. To his staff's astonishment, he gave me two hours of his time.

When I told Brother Roloff about the native missionary movement, he invited me to be his guest on *Family Altar*—his daily radio broadcast. At that time we were helping only 100 native missionaries, and Brother Roloff announced over the air that he personally was going to sponsor six more. He called me one of the "greatest missionaries he had ever met" and urged his listeners to sponsor native missionaries as well. Soon we were getting letters from all over the country.

As I read the postmarks and the letters, I realized again just how huge the United States and Canada really are. Brother Roloff was the first Christian leader I had met who had done what I knew we needed to do. He had learned how to speak to the whole nation. For weeks I prayed for him, asking God to show me how I could work with him and learn from his example.

When the answer came, it was quite different from anything I had expected. The Lord gave me an idea that I now realize was unusual, almost bizarre. I would ask Brother Roloff to loan me his mailing list and let me ask his people to sponsor a native missionary.

Trembling, I called his office and asked for another appointment. He saw me again but was very surprised at my request, telling me that he had never loaned his list to anyone—even his best friends. Many agencies had asked to rent his list, but he had always said no. I thought my cause was lost, but he said he would pray about it.

The next day he called me back, saying that the Lord had told him to give us his list. He also offered to write a letter of endorsement and interview me again on the radio broadcast at the same time the letter went out. Elated, I praised God. But I soon learned that this was only the beginning of the miracle.

The list was a fairly large one, and printing a brochure, my letter and his letter, together with the mailing, would cost more money than we had. There seemed to be only one way to get it. I would have to borrow—just this once—from the missionary funds. I figured it out again and again. If I worked it just right, I could get the money to the field with only a few weeks' delay. But I had no peace about the plan. I had always used the funds exactly as designated.

When the time came to send the regular monies to the field, I told our bookkeeper to hold the money for one day, and I prayed. Still no peace. The next day I told her to hold the money for another day, and I went back to prayer and fasting. Still no peace. I delayed it for a third day—and still God would not release me to use the missionary support funds.

I was miserable. Finally I decided I could not break the trust of our donors—even for the Lord's work. I told my secretary to go ahead and send the missionary money.

I now realize we had gone through one of the greatest tests of the ministry. This was it, my first chance to get a major increase in donors and income—but it had to be done with integrity, or not at all.

A half hour after the check had gone to the field, the telephone rang. It was from a couple whom I had met only once before at our annual banquet in Dallas. They had been praying about helping us, and God had laid me on their hearts. They asked if they could come and talk to me, and they wanted to know what I needed.

After I explained the cost involved for printing and putting out the mailing, they agreed to pick up the entire amount—nearly $20,000. Then the printer became so moved by the project that he did it for free! Plainly God had been testing me, and He miraculously showed that if we were obedient, He indeed would provide.

The artwork went to the printers and soon printed letters were sitting on skids, ready for the post office. I had prepared a special radio broadcast to coincide with the arrival of the mailing—and the broadcast tapes already had been shipped to stations in many parts of the nation.

Timing was everything. The mail had to go on Monday. It was Friday, and I had no undesignated money in the general fund for the postage. This time there was no question of borrowing the missionary money. It stayed right where it was.

I called a special prayer meeting, and we met that night in the living room of our home. Finally the Lord gave me peace. Our prayers of faith would be answered, I announced. After everyone had gone home, the telephone rang. It was one of our sponsors in Chicago. God had been speaking to her all day about giving a $5,000 gift.

"Praise God," I said.

That mailing incident proved to be another turning point in

the history of Gospel for Asia. We received many new sponsors—a double increase in the number of evangelists we were able to sponsor.

In later years, other Christian leaders, like Bob Walker of Christian Life Missions and David Mains of Chapel of the Air, would help us in similar ways. Many of the people who joined our ministry through those several early mailings have since helped expand the ministry even further, giving us a base of contacts from every state in the Union.

God had given us a clear message for the Body of Christ—a call to recover the Church's missionary mandate. In every place, I preached this same message—a prophetic cry to my brothers and sisters in Christ on behalf of the lost millions in the Two-Thirds World. Through it, thousands of believers started to change their lifestyles and conform to the demands of the Gospel.

Eight

A New Day in Missions

Several hundred dedicated believers now were supporting native missionaries. But despite this aura of success, many things broke my heart, especially the condition of American Christians. What had happened to the zeal for missions and outreach that made this nation so great? Night after night I stood before audiences, trying my best to communicate the global realities of our planet. But somehow I was not getting through. I could see their unfulfilled destiny so clearly. Why couldn't they?

Here were people of great privilege—a nation more able, more affluent and more free to act on the Great Commission than any other in all of history. Yet my audiences did not seem to comprehend this. Even more confusing to me was the fact that in personal dealings I found my hosts to be basically fair, often generous and spiritually gifted. Like the church in first-century Corinth, they appeared to excel in every spiritual blessing.

Why then, I asked the Lord, was I failing to get through? If the native missionary movement was really the will of God—and I knew it was—then why were the people so slow to respond?

Something obviously had gone wrong. Satan had sprung a trap, or perhaps many traps, on the minds of Western Christians. Plainly they had lost the Gospel mandate, abdicating the heritage of missionary outreach, the call of God that still rests on this nation.

In my prayers I began to seek a message from God that would bring a change in lifestyle to the American Church. It came over a period of weeks. And that message came loud and clear: Unless there is repentance among Christians—individually and in concert as a community of believers—an awesome judgment will fall on America.

I was certain then, and still am today, that God's loving hands of grace and forgiveness remain extended to His people. Two reasons, it appeared to me, were the cause for the current malaise that has fastened like cancer on American believers. The first is historical. The second is the unconfessed sins related to three basic iniquities: pride, unbelief and worldliness.

Historically, the Western Church lost its grip on the challenge for world missions at the end of World War II. Ever since that time, its moral mandate and vision for global outreach have continued to fade. Many average North American believers can hardly pronounce the word *missionary* without having cartoon caricatures of ridiculous little men in pith helmets pop into mind—images of cannibals with spears and huge black pots of boiling water.

Despite a valiant rear guard action by many outstanding evangelical leaders and missions, it has been impossible for the Western missionary movement to keep up with exploding populations and the new political realities of nationalism in the Two-Thirds World. Most Christians in North America still conceive of missions in terms of blond-haired, blue-eyed white people going to the dark-skinned Two-Thirds World nations. In reality, all of that changed at the end of World War II when the Western powers lost political and military control of their former colonies.

When I stand before North American audiences in churches and mission conferences, people are astonished to hear the real facts of missions today. The frontline work of missions in Asia has been taken over almost completely by indigenous missionaries. And the results are outstanding. Believers are shocked to learn that native missionaries are starting hundreds of new churches every week in the Two-Thirds World, that thousands of people a day are being converted to Christ, and that tens of thousands of well-qualified, spiritually able men and women now are ready to start more mission work if we can raise their support.

In India, which no longer permits Western missionary evangelists, more church growth and outreach are happening now than at any point in our history. China is another good example of the new realities. When the communists drove Western missionaries out and closed the churches in 1950, it seemed that Christianity was dead. In fact, most of the known leaders were imprisoned, and a whole generation of Chinese pastors was killed or disappeared in communist prisons and torture chambers.

But today communication is open again with China, and over 500,000 underground churches reportedly have sprung up during the communist persecution.[1] Estimates of the number of Christians today in China vary widely, but responsible authorities place it around 50 million, compared to 1 million when Western missionaries were driven out.[2] Again, all this has happened under the spiritual direction of the indigenous church movement.

From a historical perspective, it is not difficult to trace how Western thinking has been confused by the march of history. In the early 1950s, the destruction of the colonial missionary establishment was big news. As the doors of China, India, Myanmar, North Korea, North Vietnam and many other newly independent nations slammed shut on Western missionaries, it was natural for the traditional churches and denominational missions to assume that their day had ended.

That, of course, was in itself untrue, as evidenced by the

growth of evangelical missions in the same period. But many became convinced then that the age of missions had ended forever. Except for the annual missions appeal in most churches, many North American believers lost hope of seeing the Great Commission of Christ fulfilled on a global scale. Although it was rarely stated, the implication was this: If North American or Western European-based mission boards were not leading the way, then it could not happen.

Mission monies once used to proclaim the Gospel were more and more sidetracked into the charitable social programs toward which the new governments of the former colonies were more sympathetic. A convenient theology of missions developed that today sometimes equates social and political action with evangelism.

Many of the Western missionaries who did stay on in Asia also were deeply affected by the rise of nationalism. They began a steady retreat from evangelism and discipleship, concentrating for the most part on broadcasting, education, medical, publishing, relief and social work. Missionaries, when home in the West, continued to give the impression that indigenization meant not only the pullout of Western personnel but also the pullout of financial and other assistance.

The debate among Western leaders about the future of missions has in the meantime raged on, producing whole libraries of books and some valuable research. Regrettably, however, the overall result on the average Christian has been extremely negative. Believers today have no idea that a new day in missions has dawned or that their support of missions is more desperately needed than ever before.

True, in many cases, it no longer is possible, for political reasons, for Western missionaries to go overseas, but American believers still have a vital role in helping us in the Two-Thirds World finish the task. I praise God for the pioneer work done by Hudson Taylor and others like him who were sent by believers at home in the past. Now, in countries like India, we need instead to send financial and technical support to native evangelists and Bible teachers.

Imagine the implications of being involved in the work of the Great Commission, of getting your church and family to join with you in supporting native missions.

Picture this very possible scene. You finish your life on this earth. You arrive in heaven. There, enthroned in all His glory, is our Lord Jesus Christ. The other saints and martyrs you have read about are there: Abraham, Moses, Peter and Paul, plus great leaders from more recent times. Your family and loved ones who obeyed the Gospel are also there. They are all welcoming you into heaven. You walk around in bliss, filled with joy and praises. All the promises of the Bible are true. The streets really are gold, and the glory of God shines brightly, replacing the sun, moon and stars. It is beyond the power of any man to describe.

Then, scores of strangers whom you don't recognize start to gather around with happy smiles and outstretched hands. They embrace you with affection and gratitude.

"Thank you. . . . Thank you. . . . Thank you," they repeat in a chorus. With great surprise you ask, "What did I do? I have never seen you before."

They tell you the story of how they came to be in heaven, all because your love and concern reached out to them while they were on earth. You see that these persons come from "every tongue and tribe," just as the Bible says—from India, Bangladesh, Bhutan, Thailand and the Philippines.

"But what exactly did I do?" you ask. Then, like a replay of a videotape, your mind goes back to a day in your life on earth when a local mission coordinator came to your church. He told you about the lost millions of Asia—about the 400 million who have never heard the Gospel in India alone.[3] He told you about the desperately poor native missionaries and challenged you to support them.

"As a result of your support," the crowd of Asians continues, "one of our own—a native evangelist—came to us and preached the Gospel of the kingdom. He lived simply, just like us, speaking our language and dressed in our clothing. We were able to accept his message easily. We learned for the first time about the love of Jesus, who died on the cross for us, and how His blood redeemed us from sin, Satan and death."

As the crowd finishes, several whole families come up to you. You can see the tenderness and gratefulness on their faces as well. They join the others, taking you in their arms and thanking you again.

"How can we ever express our appreciation for the love and kindness you showed by supporting us on the earth as we struggled in the service of the Lord? Often we went without food. Our children cried for milk, but we had none to give. Unknown and forsaken by our own people, we sought to witness to our own people who had never heard the Gospel. Now they are here in eternity with us.

"In the middle of our suffering, you came into our lives with your prayers and financial support. Your help relieved us so much—making it possible for us to carry on the work of the Lord.

"We never had a chance to see you face-to-face in the world. Now we can see you here and spend all eternity rejoicing with you over the victories of the Lord."

Now Jesus Himself appears. You bow as He quotes the familiar Scripture verses to you: "I was an hungered, and ye gave me meat: I was thirsty, and ye gave me drink: I was a stranger, and ye took me in: naked, and ye clothed me. . . . Verily I say unto you, Inasmuch as ye have done it unto one of the least of these my brethren, ye have done it unto me" (Matthew 25:35–36, 40).

Is this just a fanciful story, or will it be reality for many thousands of North American Christians? I believe it could happen as Christians arrive in heaven and see how they have laid up treasure where moth and rust cannot corrupt.

Every time I stand before an audience, I try early in my message to ask two very important questions that every Christian needs to ask himself:

- Why do you think God has allowed you to be born in North America or Europe rather than among the poor masses of Africa and Asia and to be blessed with such material and spiritual abundance?

- In light of the superabundance you enjoy here, what do you think is your minimal responsibility to the untold millions of lost and suffering in the Two-Thirds World?

You have been born among the privileged elite of this world. You have so much while others have so little. Think a moment about the vast difference between your country and the nations without a Christian heritage.

- One-fourth of the world's people lives on an income of less than $1 a day—most of them in Asia.[4] The gross national income per person in South Asia is only $460 a year. Americans earn an average of 77 times more[5]—and Christian Americans, because they tend to live in the upper half of the economy, earn even more. In most countries where Gospel for Asia is serving the native missionary movement, a good wage is $1 to $3 a day. While much of the world is concerned mainly about where its next meal is coming from, affluent North Americans spend most of their wages and waking moments planning unnecessary purchases.

- People in the United States, Canada and Europe enjoy freedom of choice. Political freedoms of speech, press and assembly, freedom to worship and organize religious ministries, freedom to choose where and how to live, and freedom to organize themselves to correct injustices and problems both at home and abroad are accepted as normal.

- Leisure time and disposable income, although not written into law, free citizens of the Western world from the basic wants that make living so difficult in many other parts of the world.

- A large number of service networks in communications, education, finance, mass media and transportation are available that make it easy to effect change. Not having these services available is an enormous handicap to people in most other parts of the world.

- Finally, few domestic needs exist. Although unemployment is a serious problem in some areas, it is many times higher in nearly every country of the Two-Thirds World. How many of us can comprehend the suffering of the millions of homeless and starving people in nations like Bangladesh? Overseas the problems are on a grand scale. Some nations struggle to help themselves but still fail woefully.

This list is illustrative of the many advantages of living in the Western world where benefits have come largely because of a Christian heritage.

Nine

Is Missions an Option?

If the apostle Paul had not brought the Gospel to Europe, foundational principles such as freedom and human dignity would not be part of the American heritage. Because the Holy Spirit instructed him to turn away from Asia and go West, America has been blessed with its systems of law and economics—the principles that made it rich and free.

In addition, the United States is the only nation in the world founded by believers in Christ who made a covenant with God—dedicating a new nation to God.

Born into affluence, freedom and divine blessings, Americans should be the most thankful people on earth.

But along with the privilege comes a responsibility. The Christian must ask not only why, but also what he should do with these unearned favors.

Throughout Scripture, we see only one correct response to abundance: sharing.

God gives some people more than they need so that they can be channels of blessing to others. God desires equity between His people on a worldwide basis. That is why the early Church had no poverty.

The apostle Paul wrote to the rich Christians in Corinth, "For I mean not that other men be eased, and ye burdened: But by an equality, that now at this time your abundance

may be a supply for their want, that their abundance also
may be a supply for your want: that there may be equality"
(2 Corinthians 8:13–14).

The Bible advocates and demands that we show love for the
needy brethren. Right now, because of historical and economic
factors that none of us can control, the needy brethren are in
Asia. The wealthy brethren are in the United States, Canada and
a few other nations. The conclusion is obvious: These affluent
believers must share with the poorer churches.

"We know that we have passed from death unto life, because
we love the brethren. . . . But whoso hath this world's good,
and seeth his brother have need, and shutteth up his bowels of
compassion from him, how dwelleth the love of God in him?
My little children, let us not love in word, neither in tongue; but
in deed and in truth" (1 John 3:14, 17–18).

And, "What doth it profit, my brethren, though a man say he
hath faith, and have not works? can faith save him? If a brother
or sister be naked, and destitute of daily food, And one of you
say unto them, Depart in peace, be ye warmed and filled; not-
withstanding ye give them not those things which are needful to
the body; what doth it profit? Even so faith, if it hath not works,
is dead, being alone" (James 2:14–17).

Is missions an option—especially for superwealthy countries
like America? The biblical answer is clear. Every Christian in
America has some minimal responsibility to get involved in
helping the poor brethren in the Church in other countries.

God has not given this superabundance of blessings to
American and Canadian Christians so we can sit back and enjoy
the luxuries of this society—or even in spiritual terms, so we can
gorge ourselves on books, teaching cassettes and deeper-life conferences. He has left us on this earth to be stewards of these spiritual and material blessings, learning how to share with others
and administer our wealth to accomplish the purposes of God.

What is the bottom line? God is calling us as Christians to alter our lifestyles, to give up the nonessentials of our lives so we can better invest our wealth in the kingdom of God.

To start, I challenge believers to lay aside at least $1 a day to help support a native missionary in the Two-Thirds World. This, of course, should be over and above our present commitments to the local church and other ministries. I do not ask Christians to redirect their giving away from other ministries for native missions—but to expand their giving over and above current levels. Most people can do this.

Millions of North American and European believers can accomplish this easily by giving up cookies, cakes, sweets, coffee and other beverages. These junk foods harm our bodies anyway, and anyone can save enough in this way to help sponsor one or even two missionaries a month. Many are going beyond this and, without affecting health or happiness, are able to help sponsor several missionaries every month.

There are, of course, many other ways to get involved. Some cannot give more financially, but they can invest time in prayer and help recruit more sponsors. And a few are called to go overseas to become more directly involved.

But I would submit to you that the single most important hindrance to world evangelization right now is the lack of total involvement by the Body of Christ. I am convinced there are enough potential sponsors to support all the native missionaries needed to evangelize the Two-Thirds World.

The native missionary movement is relatively new, and many Christians still have not been challenged to participate, but that is superficial. The real truth is much more basic—and more deadly. The three major reasons why the Body of Christ falls short in facilitating world evangelization are the sins of pride, unbelief and worldliness.

Ask the average Christian why the Lord destroyed Sodom,

and he or she will cite the city's gross immorality. Ezekiel, however, reveals the real reason in chapter 16, verses 49 and 50: "Behold, this was the iniquity of thy sister Sodom, pride, fulness of bread, and abundance of idleness was in her and in her daughters, neither did she strengthen the hand of the poor and needy. And they were haughty, and committed abomination before me: therefore I took them away as I saw good."

Sodom refused to aid the needy poor because of pride. We are caught up in a national pride similar to Sodom's. Yes, selfishness and perversion come from that pride, but we need to see that pride is the real root. Deal with that root and you cut off a multitude of sins before they have a chance to grow.

One night while speaking at a church missionary conference, I was asked to meet privately with the church council to give my reaction to a new mission program they were considering. I already had preached and was very tired. I did not feel like sitting in a board meeting. The meeting, attended by 22 persons, began in the usual way, more like a corporate board meeting at IBM or General Motors than a church board.

The presenter made an impressive, business-like proposal. The scheme involved shifting "third country nationals" from Asia to a mission field in Latin America. It was very futuristic and sounded like a major leap in missions, but warning lights and bells were going off in my mind. To me it sounded like 19th-century colonial missionary practice dressed in a different disguise.

The Lord spoke to me clearly: "Son, tonight you must speak to people who are so self-sufficient they've never asked Me about this plan. They think I'm helpless."

When the chairman of the church council finally called on me to respond with my opinion of the proposal, I stood and read certain parts of Matthew 28:18-20: "All power is given unto me in heaven and in earth. Go ye therefore, and teach all nations . . . to observe all things whatsoever I have commanded you: and, lo, I am with you alway. . . ."

Then I closed my Bible and paused, looking each one in the eyes.

"If He is with you," I said, "then you will represent Him—not just be like Him—but you will exercise His authority. Where is the power of God in this plan?"

I did not need to say much. The Holy Spirit anointed my words, and everyone seemed to understand.

"How often have you met for prayer?" I asked rhetorically. "How long since you have had an entire day of prayer to seek God's mind about your mission strategy?" From their eyes it was easy to see they had prayed little about their mission budget, which was then in the hundreds of thousands of dollars.

The discussion went on until 1:30 in the morning, but with a new sense of repentance in the room.

"Brother K.P.," said the leader to me afterward, "you have destroyed everything we were trying to do tonight, but now we're ready to wait on God for His plan."

That kind of humility will bring the Church back into the center of God's will and global plan. Churches today are not experiencing the power and anointing of God in their ministries because they do not have the humility to wait on Him. Because of that sin, the world remains largely unreached.

So little of evangelical Christian work is done in total dependence upon the living God. Like our brothers and sisters in that big church, we have devised methods, plans and techniques to "do" God's work. Those involved apparently sense no need to pray or be filled with the Holy Spirit to do the work of Jesus.

How far we have drifted from the faith of the apostles and the prophets! What a tragedy when the techniques of the world and its agents are brought into the sanctuary of God. Only when we are emptied of our own self-sufficiency can God use us. When a church or a mission board spends more time in consultation, planning and committee meetings than in prayer, it is a clear indication the members have lost touch with the supernatural and have ended up, in Watchman Nee's words, "serving the house of God and forgot the Lord Himself."

Part of the sin of pride is a subtle but deep racism. As I travel, I often hear innocent-sounding questions such as, "How do we know that the native church is ready to handle the funds?" or, "What kind of training have the native missionaries had?"

So long as such questions are based on a sincere desire for good stewardship, they are commendable, but in many cases I have found the intent of the questions to be much less honorable. Westerners refuse to trust Asians the way they trust their own people. If we're satisfied that a certain native missionary is truly called to the Gospel, we have to trust God and turn our stewardship over to him and his elders just as we would to another brother in our own culture. To expect to continue controlling the use of money and the ministry overseas from our foreign-based mission board is an extension of colonialism. It adds an unbiblical element, which only humiliates and weakens the native missionaries in the long run.

Christians need to learn that they are not giving their money to native workers, but God's money to His work overseas.

Here are some further manifestations of pride: Instead of glorifying two-fisted fighters in the John Wayne tradition of American folk heroes, Christians would do well to sit still until the power of God is manifested in their Christian activities.

Churches need to develop the quiet disciplines they have lost—practices such as contemplation, fasting, listening, meditation, prayer, silence, Scripture memory, submission and reflection.

Many Christian leaders are caught up in secondary issues that sap their time and energy. I will never forget preaching in one church where the pastor had turned defending the King James translation of the Bible into a crusade. Not only does he spend most of his pulpit time upholding it—but thousands of dollars go to printing books, tracts and pamphlets advocating the exclusive use of this one translation.

In the years I have lived and worked in the United States, I have watched believers and whole congregations get caught up in all kinds of similar crusades and causes that, while not necessarily bad in themselves, end up taking our eyes off obedience to Christ. And in this sense, they become anti-Christ. Red-hot issues burning across the horizon—such as inerrancy, charismatic gifts, the latest revelations of itinerant teachers or secular humanism, or whatever new issue raises its head tomorrow—need to be kept in their proper perspective. There always will be new dragons to slay, but we must not let these side battles keep us from our main task of building and expanding the kingdom of God.

When I go to Asia, I see our churches and theologians there being just as violently divided over a different set of issues, and through this I have come to realize that many times these doctrinal divisions are being used by the evil one to keep us preoccupied with something other than the Gospel.

We are driven by powerful egos always to be right. We are often slaves to a strong tendency to "have it our way." All of these are manifestations of pride. The opposite of that is the servanthood and humble sacrifice commanded by Christ. Making a sacrifice for one of the unknown brethren—supporting his work to a strange people in a strange place, using methods that are a mystery to you—does take humility. But supporting the native brethren must begin with this kind of commitment to humility and must continue in the same spirit. Sadly, our pride all too often stands in the way of progress.

Ten

God Is Withholding Judgment

Beware of boasters. They are usually covering up something. One of the great boasts of many Western evangelical Christians is their devotion to the Scriptures. It is hard to find a church that does not at one time or another brag about being "Bible believing." When I first came here, I made the mistake of taking that description at face value.

But I have come to see that many evangelical Christians do not really believe the Word of God, especially when it talks about hell and judgment. Instead, they selectively accept only the portions that allow them to continue living in their current lifestyles.

It is painful to think about hell and judgment. I understand why preachers do not like to talk about it, because I don't either. It is so much easier to preach that "God loves you and has a wonderful plan for your life" or to focus on the many delightful aspects of "possibility thinking" and the "word of faith" that brings health, wealth and happiness. The grace and love of God are pleasant subjects, and no one more beautifully demonstrated them than our Lord Jesus. Yet in His earthly ministry, He made more references to hell and judgment than He did to heaven. Jesus lived with the reality of hell, and He died on Calvary because He knew it was real and coming to everyone who doesn't turn to God in this life.

Believers are willing to accept the concept of heaven, but they look the other way when they come to passages in the Bible about hell. Very few seem to believe that those who die without Christ are going to a place where they will be tormented forever and ever in a bottomless pit where the fire is not quenched and they are separated from God and His love for all eternity without any chance of return.

If we knew the horrors of the potential judgment that hangs over us—if we really believed in what is coming—how differently we would live. Why aren't Christians living in obedience to God? Because of their unbelief.

Why did Eve fall into sin? Because she did not truly believe in the judgment—that death really would come if she ate what God forbade. This is the same reason many continue in lives of sin and disobedience.

The Great Depression and recent recessions are only a slap on the wrist compared to the poverty that lies ahead—let alone the bombs, disease and natural calamities. But God is withholding judgment now to give us time to repent.

Unfortunately for millions in the Two-Thirds World, it will be too late unless we can reach them before they slip off the edge into eternal darkness.

For years I have struggled with making this a reality in our meetings. Finally I found a way.

I ask my listeners to hold their wrists and find their pulse. Then I explain that every beat they feel represents the death of someone in Asia who has died and gone to eternal hell without ever hearing the Good News of Jesus Christ even once.

"What if one of those beats represented your own mother?" I ask. "Your own father, your spouse, your child . . . you yourself?"

The millions of Asians who are dying and going to hell are people for whom Christ died. We say we believe it—but what are we doing to act on that faith? Without works, faith is dead.

No one should go to hell today without hearing about the Lord Jesus. To me this is an atrocity much worse than the death camps of Hitler's Germany or Stalin's Russia. As horrible as the 1.3 million abortions are in the United States each year, the eternal loss of multiplied millions of additional souls every year is the greatest preventable tragedy of our times.

If only a small percentage of the 80 million people who claim to be born-again Christians in this country were to sponsor a native missionary, we could have literally hundreds of thousands of evangelists reaching the lost villages of Asia. When we look at the unfinished Great Commission and compare it to our personal lifestyles—or to the activity calendars of our churches and organizations—how can we explain our disobedience? We must see a great repentance from the sin of our unbelief in God's judgment.

C.T. Studd, the famous British athlete and founder of Worldwide Evangelization Crusade, was one who gave up all his achievements in this life for Christ's sake. He was challenged to his commitment by an article written by an atheist. That article in part said:

> If I firmly believed, as millions say they do, that the knowledge and practice of religion in this life influences destiny in another, then religion would mean to me everything.
>
> I would cast away earthly enjoyments as dross, earthly cares as follies, and earthly thoughts and feelings as vanity. Religion would be my first waking thought and my last image before sleep sank me into unconsciousness. I should labor in its cause alone.
>
> I would take thought for the morrow of eternity alone. I would esteem one soul gained for heaven worth a life of suffering.
>
> Earthly consequences would never stay my hand, or seal my lips. Earth, its joys and its griefs, would occupy no moment of my thoughts. I would strive to look upon eternity alone, and on the immortal souls around me, soon to be everlastingly happy

or everlastingly miserable.

I would go forth to the world and preach to it in season and out of season, and my text would be:

"WHAT SHALL IT PROFIT A MAN IF HE GAIN THE WHOLE WORLD AND LOSE HIS OWN SOUL?"[1]

Another iniquity plaguing the Western Church is worldliness.

Once, on a 2,000-mile auto trip across the American West, I made it a point to listen to Christian radio all along the way. What I heard revealed much about the secret motivations that drive many Christians. Some of the broadcasts would have been hilarious if they weren't exploiting the gullible—hawking health, wealth and success in the name of Christianity.

- Some speakers offered holy oil and lucky charms to those who sent in money and requested them.

- Some speakers offered prayer cloths that had blessed believers with $70,000 to $100,000, new cars, houses and health.

- One speaker said he would mail holy soap he had blessed. If used with his instructions, it would wash away bad luck, evil friends and sickness. Again he promised "plenty of money" and everything else the user wanted.

Such con games bring a smile to our lips, but the same basic package is marketed with more sophistication at every level of this society. Christian magazines, TV shows and church services often put the spotlight on famous athletes, beauty queens, businessmen and politicians who "make it in the world and have Jesus too!"

Today Christian values are defined almost totally by success as it is promoted by Madison Avenue advertising. Even many

Christian ministries gauge their effectiveness by the standards of Harvard MBAs.

Jesus said the heart is where the treasures are kept. So what can we say about many evangelical Christians? Getting into debt for cars, homes and furnishings that probably are not needed and sacrificing family, church and health for corporate promotions and career advancement—I believe all this is deception, engineered by the god of this world to ensnare and destroy effective Christians and to keep them from sharing the Gospel with those who need it.

"Love not the world," says John in his first epistle, "neither the things that are in the world. If any man love the world, the love of the Father is not in him. For all that is in the world, the lust of the flesh, and the lust of the eyes, and the pride of life, is not of the Father, but is of the world. And the world passeth away, and the lust thereof: but he that doeth the will of God abideth for ever" (1 John 2:15–17).

The typical media testimony goes something like this: "I was sick and broke, a total failure. Then I met Jesus. Now everything is fine; my business is booming, and I am a great success."

It sounds wonderful. Be a Christian and get that bigger house and a boat and vacation in the Holy Land.

But if that were really God's way, it would put some Christians behind the Iron Curtain and in the Two-Thirds World in a pretty bad light. Their testimonies often go something like this:

"I was happy. I had everything—prestige, recognition, a good job, and a happy wife and children. Then I gave my life to Jesus Christ. Now I am in Siberia, having lost my family, wealth, reputation, job and health.

"Here I live, lonely, deserted by friends. I cannot see the face of my wife and dear children. My crime is that I love Jesus."

What about the heroes of the faith down through the ages? The apostles laid down their lives for the Lord. Christian martyrs have written their names on every page of history.

In Russia, Ivan Moiseyev was tortured and killed within two years of meeting Jesus. In China, Watchman Nee spent 20 years in prison and finally died in bondage.

When Sadhu Sundar Singh, born and raised in a rich Sikh's home in Punjab, became a Christian, his own family tried to poison him and banished him from their home. He lost his inheritance and walked away with one piece of clothing on his body. Yet, following his Master, he made millions truly rich through faith in Christ.

The native missionaries supported by Gospel for Asia often suffer for their commitment also. Coming from non-Christian backgrounds, they often are literally thrown out of their homes, lose their jobs and are beaten and chased from their villages when they accept Christ.

They faithfully serve Christ daily, suffering untold hardships because Jesus promised His followers, "In the world ye shall have tribulation: but be of good cheer; I have overcome the world" (John 16:33). What He promised were trials and tribulations. But we can face them because we know He already has won the battle. God does promise to meet our physical needs. And He does, indeed, bless His children materially. But He blesses us for a purpose—not so we can squander those resources on ourselves but so we can be good stewards, using our resources wisely to win the lost to God's saving grace.

The Scripture tells us, "Whoso hath this world's good, and seeth his brother have need, and shutteth up his bowels of compassion from him, how dwelleth the love of God in him?" (1 John 3:17).

As A.W. Tozer, noted Christian and Missionary Alliance pastor and author, once said,

There is no doubt that the possessive clinging to things is one of the most harmful habits in life. Because it is so natural, it is rarely recognized for the evil that it is. But its outworking is tragic. This ancient curse will not go out painlessly. The tough old miser within us will not lie down and die obedient to our command. He must be torn out, torn out of our hearts like a plant from the soil; he must be extracted in blood and agony like a tooth from the jaw. He must be expelled from our souls in violence as Christ expelled the money changers from the temple.[2]

Many Western believers are the rich young rulers of our day. Jesus is saying to them, "If thou wilt be perfect, go and sell that thou hast, and give to the poor, and thou shalt have treasure in heaven: and come and follow me" (Matthew 19:21).

Eleven

Why Should I Make Waves?

By the end of 1981, Gospel for Asia appeared to be gaining acceptance; people from all over the United States and Canada were beginning to share in the ministry of equipping native missionaries to evangelize in their own countries.

As Gisela and our office staff in Dallas worked to assign our new sponsors to native missionaries, I felt led of the Lord to plan a road tour of 14 Texas towns to meet personally with new supporters. Calling ahead, I introduced myself and thanked the people for taking on the sponsorship of a native missionary.

I was stunned by the response. Most of the people had heard me on the radio and appeared thrilled with the idea of meeting me. In every town, someone offered me lodging and made arrangements for me to speak in small house meetings and churches. People were referring to me in a new way—as the president and director of an important missionary organization. Far from being pleased, I was more terrified than ever—afraid that I would fail or be rejected.

But with the meetings booked solid and the publicity out, an unreasonable fear took over. A weariness settled upon me. As the day for my departure came closer, I looked for excuses to cancel or postpone the whole venture.

"My family and the office need me more," I argued. "Besides, I'll be driving alone. It's dangerous and difficult—I should really wait until someone can go with me."

Just when I had almost talked myself out of going, the Lord spoke to me in an unmistakable voice during my personal morning devotion. As on other occasions, it was just as if He were in the room with me.

"My sheep hear My voice," said the Lord, using His words from John 10, "and I know them and they follow Me: My sheep follow Me because they know My voice."

I did not need an interpretation; the message was clear. The trip had been ordained by Him. He had arranged it and opened the doors. I needed to picture myself as a little lamb and follow my Shepherd over the miles. He would go ahead of me to every church and every home in which I would stay.

It turned out to be a heavenly two weeks. In every home and church, I had delightful fellowship with our new friends—and we added a number of supporters as a result.

The church in Victoria, Texas, was almost my last stop, and the Lord had a surprise waiting for me there. But He had to prepare me first.

As I drove from town to town, I had time alone in the car for the Lord to deal with me on several issues that would impact the future of the mission and my own walk with Him.

One issue involved one of the most far-reaching policy decisions I ever would make. For some years I had suffered deep pain over what appeared to be massive imbalance between our busyness with maintaining Christian institutions, like hospitals and schools, and the proclamation of the Gospel. Both in India and in my travels around Western countries, I constantly uncovered a preoccupation with so-called "ministry" activities operated by Christian workers, financed by church monies, but with little else to distinguish them as Christian.

Far too much of the resources of North American missions is spent on things not related to the primary goal of church planting. Wagner, in his book *On the Crest of the Wave*, says, "I have before me a recent list of openings in a . . . mission agency which will go unnamed. Of 50 different categories, only two relate to evangelism, both focused on youth. The rest of the categories include, among others, agronomists, music teachers, nurses, automobile mechanics, secretaries, electronics professors, and ecologists."[1]

Social concern is a natural fruit of the Gospel. But to put it first is to put the cart before the horse; and from experience, we have seen it fail in India for more than 200 years. It was an attempt to exclusively concentrate on people's obvious social needs.

Yet while I realized the intrinsic nature of the Gospel involved caring for the poor, I knew the priority was giving them the Gospel. Meeting their needs was a means to share the love of Christ so they would be saved for eternity.

I did not go this route because I felt other Christian charities and ministries of compassion were wrong in showing the love of Christ. No, many were doing a wonderful job. But I felt the local church should be the center for outreach, and we needed to bring the balance back.

I did not publicly tell anyone about my decision. I knew this subject would be controversial, and I was afraid others would think I was being judgmental, a "fighting fundy" reactionary, or a fanatic. I only wanted to help the native missionary movement, and I reasoned that getting into arguments over mission strategy would be counterproductive.

Then came Victoria, Texas.

My presentation went nicely. I showed the GFA slides and made an impassioned plea for our work. I explained the philosophy of our ministry, giving the biblical reasons why the heathen are lost unless native missionaries go to them.

Suddenly, I felt the Spirit prompting me to talk about the

dangers of the humanist social gospel. I paused for the briefest moment, then went on without mentioning it. I just did not have the courage. I might make enemies everywhere. People would think I was an unloving fool, a spoiler of Christian work who did not even care about the hungry, naked, needy and suffering. Why should I make waves? I managed to get through my presentation, and feeling relieved, I opened up the meeting to questions.

But the Holy Spirit was not about to let me off the hook.

From far in the back of the room, a tall man—at least "six foot three" as they say in Texas—came walking steadily up the aisle, looking bigger and bigger as he came closer to me. I did not know who he was or what he had to say, but I felt instinctively that God had sent him. When he reached me, he wrapped a huge arm around my skinny shoulders and said some words I still can hear ringing today: "This man here, our brother, is fearful and afraid to speak the truth . . . and he's struggling with it." I felt my face and neck getting hot with guilt. How did this big cowboy know that? But it got worse, and I was about to see proof that the Spirit of the living God was really using this tall Texan to deliver a powerful confirmation and rebuke to me.

"The Lord has led you in ways others have not walked and shown you things others have not seen," he went on. "The souls of millions are at stake. You must speak the truth about the misplaced priority on the mission field. You must call the Body of Christ to return to the task of preaching salvation and snatching souls from hell."

I felt like a zero, yet this was undeniably a miraculous prophecy inspired by God, confirming both my disobedience and the very message God had called me to preach fearlessly. But my humiliation and liberation were not over yet.

"The Lord has asked me," the tall man said, "to call the elders up here to pray for you that this fear of man will leave you."

Suddenly I felt like even less than a zero. I had been introduced as a great mission leader; now I felt like a little lamb. I wanted to defend myself. I did not feel as if I were being controlled by a spirit of fear; I felt that I was just acting logically to protect the interests of our mission. But I submitted anyway, feeling a little ridiculous, as the elders crowded around me to pray for an anointing of power on my preaching ministry.

Something happened. I felt the power of God envelop me. A few minutes later I got up from my knees a changed man, released from the bondage of fear that had gripped me. All doubts were gone: God had placed a burden on my life to deliver this message.

Since that day I have insisted we recover the genuine Gospel of Jesus—that balanced New Testament message that begins not with the fleshly needs of people, but with the plan and wisdom of God—"born-again" conversion that leads to righteousness, sanctification and redemption. Any "mission" that springs from "the base things of the world" is a betrayal of Christ and is what the Bible calls "another gospel." It cannot save or redeem people either as individuals or as a society. We preach a Gospel, not for the years of time alone, but for eternity.

The only trouble with half-truths is that they contain within them full lies. Such is the case with this declaration issued at the 1928 Jerusalem Conference of the International Missionary Council: "Our fathers were impressed with the horror that men should die without Christ; we were equally impressed with the horror that they should live without Christ."

Out of such rhetoric—usually delivered passionately by an ever-growing number of sincere humanists within our churches—come myriads of worldly social programs. Such efforts really snatch salvation and true redemption from the poor—condemning them to eternity in hell.

Of course, there is a basic truth to the statement. Living this life without Christ is an existence of horrible emptiness, one that offers no hope or meaning. But the subtle humanist lie it hides places the accent on the welfare of this present physical life.

What few realize is that this teaching grew out of the influence of 19th-century humanists, the very same men who gave us modern atheism, communism and the many other modern philosophies that deny God's sovereignty in the affairs of men. They are, as the Bible says, "antichrists."

Modern man unconsciously holds highest the humanistic ideals of happiness, freedom and economic, cultural and social progress for all mankind. This secular view says there is no God, heaven or hell; there is just one chance at life, so do what makes you most happy. It also teaches that "since all men are brothers," we should work for that which contributes toward the welfare of all men.

This teaching—so attractive on the surface—has entered our churches in many ways, creating a man-centered and man-made gospel based on changing the outside and social status of man by meeting his physical needs. The cost is his eternal soul.

The so-called humanist gospel—which isn't really the "good news" at all—is called by many names. Some argue for it in familiar biblical and theological terms; some call it the "social gospel" or the "holistic gospel," but the label is not important.

You can tell the humanist gospel because it refuses to admit that the basic problem of humanity is not physical, but spiritual. The humanist won't tell you sin is the root cause of all human suffering. The latest emphasis of the movement starts by arguing that we should operate mission outreach that provides "care for the whole man," but it ends up providing help for only the body and soul—ignoring the spirit.

Because of this teaching, many churches and mission societies now are redirecting their limited outreach funds and personnel away from evangelism to something vaguely called "social concern." Today the majority of Christian missionaries find themselves primarily involved in feeding the hungry, caring for the sick through hospitals, housing the homeless or other kinds of relief and development work. In extreme cases, among nonevangelicals, the logical direction of this thinking can lead to organizing guerrilla forces, planting terrorist bombs or less extreme activities like sponsoring dance and aerobic exercise classes. This is done in the name of Jesus and supposedly is based on His command to go into all the world and preach the Gospel to every creature. The mission of the Church, as defined by these humanists, can be almost anything except winning people to Christ and discipling them.

History already has taught us that this gospel—without the blood of Christ, conversion and the cross—is a total failure. In China and India we have had seven generations of this teaching, brought to us by the British missionaries in a slightly different form in the middle of the 19th-century. My people have watched the English hospitals and schools come and go without any noticeable effect on either our churches or society.

Watchman Nee, an early Chinese native missionary, put his finger on the problem in a series of lectures delivered in the years before World War II. Read some of his comments on such efforts, as recorded in the book *Love Not the World:*

> When material things are under spiritual control they fulfill their proper subordinate role. Released from that restraint they manifest very quickly the power that lies behind them. The law of their nature asserts itself, and their worldly character is proved by the course they take.
>
> The spread of missionary enterprise in our present era gives us an opportunity to test this principle in the religious institutions of our day and of our land. Over a century ago the Church set out to establish in China schools and hospitals with a definite spiritual tone and an evangelistic objective. In those early days

not much importance was attached to the buildings, while considerable emphasis was placed on the institutions' role in the proclamation of the Gospel. Ten or 15 years ago you could go over the same ground and in many places find much larger and finer institutions on those original sites, but compared with the earlier years, far fewer converts. And by today many of those splendid schools and colleges have become purely educational centers, lacking in any truly evangelistic motive at all, while to an almost equal extent, many of the hospitals exist now solely as places merely of physical and no longer spiritual healing. The men who initiated them had, by their close walk with God, held those institutions steadfastly into His purpose; but when they passed away, the institutions themselves quickly gravitated toward worldly standards and goals, and in doing so classified themselves as "things of the world." We should not be surprised that this is so.

Nee continues to expand on the theme, this time addressing the problem of emergency relief efforts for the suffering:

In the early chapters of the Acts we read how a contingency arose which led the Church to institute relief for the poorer saints. That urgent institution of social service was clearly blessed of God, but it was of a temporary nature. Do you exclaim, "How good if it had continued?" Only one who does not know God would say that. Had those relief measures been prolonged indefinitely they would certainly have veered in the direction of the world, once the spiritual influence at work in their inception was removed. It is inevitable.

For there is a distinction between the Church of God's building, on the one hand, and on the other, those valuable social and charitable by-products that are thrown off by it from time to time through the faith and vision of its members. The latter, for all their origin in spiritual vision, possess in themselves a power of independent survival which the Church of God does not have. They are works which the faith of God's children may initiate and pioneer, but which once the way has been shown and the professional standard set, can be readily sustained or imitated by men of the world quite apart from that faith.

The Church of God, let me repeat, never ceases to be dependent upon the life of God for its maintenance.[2]

The trouble with the social gospel, even when it is clothed in religious garb and operating within Christian institutions, is that it seeks to fight what is basically a spiritual warfare with weapons of the flesh.

Our battle is not against flesh and blood or symptoms of sin like poverty and sickness. It is against Lucifer and countless demons who struggle day and night to take human souls into a Christless eternity.

As much as we want to see hundreds and thousands of new missionaries go into all the dark places, if they don't know what they are there to do, the result will be fatal. We must send soldiers into battle with the right weapons and understanding of the enemy's tactics.

If we intend to answer man's greatest problem—his separation from the eternal God—with rice handouts, then we are throwing a drowning man a board instead of helping him out of the water.

A spiritual battle fought with spiritual weapons will produce eternal victories. This is why we insist upon restoring a right balance to Gospel outreach. The accent must first and always be on evangelism and discipleship.

Twelve

Good Works and the Gospel

To keep Christian missions off balance, Satan has woven a masterful web of deceit and lies. He has invented a whole system of appealing half-truths to confuse the Church and ensure that millions will go to hell without ever receiving the Gospel. Here are a few of his more common inventions:

One, how can we preach the Gospel to a man with an empty stomach? A man's stomach has nothing to do with his heart's condition of being a rebel against the holy God. A rich American on Fifth Avenue in New York City or a poor beggar on the streets of Bombay are both rebels against God Almighty, according to the Bible. The result of this lie is the fact that, during the past 100 years, the majority of mission money has been invested in social work. I am not saying we should not care for the poor and needy. The issue I am taking to task is losing our primary focus of preaching the Gospel.

Two, social work—meeting only the physical needs of man—is mission work; in fact, it is equal to preaching. Luke 16:19–25 tells us the pitiful story of the rich man and Lazarus. Of what benefit were the possessions of the rich man? He could not pay his way out of hell. His riches could not comfort him. The rich man had lost everything, including his soul. What about Lazarus? He didn't have any possessions to lose, but he had made preparations for his soul. What was more important during their time on earth? Was it the care for the "body temple" or the immortal soul? "For what is a man advantaged, if he gain the whole world, and lose himself, or be cast away?" (Luke 9:25).

It is a crime against lost humanity to go in the name of Christ and missions just to do social work yet neglect calling men to repent—to give up their idols and rebellion—and follow Christ with all their hearts.

Three, they will not listen to the Gospel unless we offer them something else first. I have sat on the streets of Bombay with beggars—poor men who very soon would die. In sharing the Gospel with many of them, I told them I had no material goods to give them, but I came to offer eternal life. I began to share the love of Jesus who died for their souls, about the many mansions in my Father's house (John 14:2) and the fact that they can go there to hunger and thirst no more. The Lord Jesus will wipe away every tear from their eyes, I said. They shall no longer be in any debt. There shall no longer be any mourning, crying or pain (Revelation 7:16, 21:4).

What a joy it was to see some of them opening their hearts after hearing about the forgiveness of sin they can find in Jesus! That is exactly what the Bible teaches in Romans 10:17, "So then faith cometh by hearing, and hearing by the word of God."

Substituting a bowl of rice for the Holy Spirit and the Word of God will never save a soul and will rarely change the attitude of a man's heart. We will not even begin to make a dent in the kingdom of darkness until we lift up Christ with all the authority, power and revelation that is given to us in the Bible.

In few countries is the failure of Christian humanism more apparent than in Thailand. There, after 150 years of missionaries showing marvelous social compassion, Christians still make up only two percent of the entire population.[1]

Self-sacrificing missionaries probably have done more to modernize the country than any other single force. Thailand owes to missionaries its widespread literacy, first printing press, first university, first hospital, first doctor and almost every other benefit of education and science. In every area, including trade and diplomacy, Christian missionaries put the needs of the host nation first and helped usher in the 20th century. Meanwhile, millions have slipped into eternity without the Lord. They died more educated, better governed and healthier—but they died without Christ and are bound for hell.

What went wrong? Were these missionaries not dedicated enough? Were their doctrines unscriptural? Perhaps they did not believe in eternal hell or eternal heaven. Did they lack Bible training, or did they just not go out to preach to the lost? Did they shift their priorities from being interested in saving souls to relieving human suffering? I know now it was probably a little of all of these things.

While I was seeking answers to these questions, I met poor, often minimally educated, native brothers involved in Gospel work in pioneer areas. They had nothing material to offer the people to whom they preached—no agricultural training and no medical relief or school program. But hundreds of souls were saved, and in a few years, a number of churches were established. What were these brothers doing right to achieve such results, while the others with many more advantages had failed?

The answer lies in our basic understanding of what mission work is all about. There is nothing wrong with charitable acts—but they are *not* to be confused with preaching the Gospel. Feeding programs can save a man dying from hunger. Medical aid can prolong life and fight disease. Housing projects can make this temporary life more comfortable—but only the Gospel of Jesus Christ can save a soul from a life of sin and an eternity in hell!

To look into the sad eyes of a hungry child or see the wasted life of a drug addict is only to see the evidence of Satan's hold on this world. He is the ultimate enemy of mankind, and he will do everything within his considerable power to kill and destroy people. But to try to fight this terrible enemy with only physical weapons is like fighting tanks with stones.

When commerce had been established with the Fiji Islanders, a merchant who was an atheist and skeptic landed on the island to do business. He was talking to the Fijian chief and noticed a Bible and some other paraphernalia of religion around the house.

"What a shame," he said, "that you have listened to this foolish nonsense of the missionaries."

The chief replied, "Do you see the large white stone over there? That is a stone where just a few years ago we used to smash the heads of our victims to get at their brains. Do you see that large oven over there? That is the oven where just a few years ago we used to bake the bodies of our victims before we feasted upon them. Had we not listened to what you call the nonsense of those missionaries, I assure you that your head would already be smashed on that rock and your body would be baking in that oven."

There is no record of the merchant's response to that explanation of the importance of the Gospel of Christ.

When God changes the heart and spirit, the physical changes also. If you want to meet the needs of the poor in this world, there is no better place to start than by preaching the Gospel. It has done more to lift up the downtrodden, the hungry and the needy than all the social programs ever imagined by secular humanists.

These terrible words of Jesus should haunt our souls: "Ye compass sea and land to make one proselyte, and when he is made, ye make him twofold more the child of hell than yourselves" (Matthew 23:15). A.W. Tozer said it well in his book *Of God and Man:* "To spread an effete, degenerate brand of Christianity to pagan lands is not to fulfill the commandment of Christ or discharge our obligation to the heathen."[2]

Just before China was taken over by the communists, one communist officer made a revealing statement to a missionary, John Meadows: "You missionaries have been in China for over a hundred years, but you have not won China to your cause. You lament the fact that there are uncounted millions who have never heard the name of your God. Nor do they know anything of your Christianity. But we communists have been in China less than 10 years, and there is not a Chinese who does not know . . . has not heard the name of Stalin . . . or something of communism. . . . We have filled China with our doctrine.

"Now let me tell you why you have failed and we have succeeded," the officer continued. "You have tried to win the attention of masses by building churches, missions, mission hospitals, schools and what not. But we communists have printed our message and spread our literature all over China. Someday we will drive you missionaries out of our country, and we will do it by the means of the printed page."

Today, of course, John Meadows is out of China. The communists were true to their word. They won China and drove out the missionaries. Indeed, what missionaries failed to do in 100 years, the communists did in 10. One Christian leader said that if the Church had spent as much time on preaching the Gospel as it did on hospitals, orphanages, schools and rest homes—needful though they were—the Bamboo Curtain would not exist today.

The tragedy of China is being repeated today in other countries. When we allow a mission activity to focus only on the physical needs of man without the correct spiritual balance, we are participating in a program that ultimately will fail.

However, this does not mean that we must not be involved in compassion-type ministries that reach out to the poor, needy and hurting people all around us. In the next chapter, I will explain this further—our responsibility to the poor, suffering needy in our generation.

Thirteen

Hope Has Many Names

The question is, what *does* the Bible say about social justice and compassion? What is the Church's role in these matters?

Clearly, by simply looking at Christ's example of how He lived on this earth, we are not to neglect the needs of suffering humanity.

When Jesus came, He not only fed people's souls with the truths of heaven and Him as the Bread of Life, but He filled their stomachs with fish and bread and wine as well.

He opened not only the eyes of people's hearts to see the truth, but also their physical eyes, restoring their sight so they could see the world around them.

He strengthened the faith of the weak, while strengthening the legs of the lame.

He who came to breathe eternal life into a valley of dry, dead souls also breathed life into the widow's son, raising him up once more (see Luke 7:11–15).

It was not one or the other—it was *both*, and both for the glory of God.

This example of ministry carries all throughout the Bible. Look back through the Old Testament and you will see a strong emphasis placed on compassion toward the needy and social justice for the downtrodden and poor. God demanded the care and protection of all those who were oppressed (see Leviticus

19:18; Isaiah 1:17, 58:10–11), and some of the most terrible judgment fell upon the cities of Sodom and Gomorrah for the way that they exploited the poor and needy.

In Matthew 22:38–40, Jesus clearly marked the Christian's social responsibility when He said that loving God is the first and greatest commandment and "the second is like unto it, Thou shalt love thy neighbor as thyself. On these *two* commandments hang all the law and the prophets" (emphasis mine).

All the Law and Prophets are summed up in *both*—loving God and loving others. It was not one or the other—but again *both*, for the glory of God.

We cannot say we love others if we ignore their spiritual needs. Just the same, we cannot say we love others if we ignore their physical needs. Jesus came for both.

Indeed, Jesus has shown how the physical suffering of humanity brought many to call upon Him as the Savior of their soul.

In John 20:30–31 we are told, "Many other signs truly did Jesus in the presence of his disciples . . . that ye might believe that Jesus is the Christ, the Son of God; and that believing ye might have life through his name." The Gospel shows that it was the sick, the demon possessed, the hungry and the poor who came to Jesus and whose lives were changed by His healing touch. Jesus Himself declared that He had come to preach the Good News to the poor, the prisoners, the blind and the oppressed (see Luke 4:18).

Through the many who were healed from horrible diseases and set free from satanic bondage, Jesus showed Himself as the only One able to save their souls from sin and death. The mercy ministries Jesus did were not an end in themselves, but were rather a means. And it is the same today.

Yet as I mentioned in the previous chapter, we must not misunderstand (or replace) evangelism for social action. The Great

Commission is not a mandate for political liberation.

Many who are familiar with the ministry of Gospel for Asia know that first and foremost we are committed to planting churches and making new disciples. Our concern has always been evangelism and church planting, never to be replaced by social work alone.

The salvation of souls and making of disciples have been our aim and goal in all things, the ruler by which all ministry opportunities are measured. But this in no way means that we do not care about the physical suffering of those to whom we seek to minister.

Our spirits, which are eternal and infinitely more precious than the whole physical world, are contained in perishable, physical bodies. And throughout the Scripture, we see that God used the felt needs of the body to draw people to Himself. Truly, the needs of suffering men, women and children in this world are great—especially in the 10/40 Window.

Calcutta alone is home to more than 100,000 street children who know not mother or father, nor love and care. They are not just a number or statistic—they are real children. Though nameless and faceless on the streets where they live, each one was created with love and is known by God.

It is doubtful they've ever held a toothbrush or a bar of soap; they've never eaten an ice-cream cone or cradled a doll. The child laborers of South Asia toil in fireworks, carpet and match factories; quarries and coal mines; rice fields, tea plantations and pastures. Because they are exposed to dust, toxic fumes and pesticides, their health is compromised; their bodies are crippled from carrying heavy weights. Some are bonded laborers, enslaved to their tasks by family poverty.

According to the Human Rights Watch, this is life for 60 to 115 million children in South Asia. In the Indian state of Tamil Nadu, nine-year-old Lakshmi works in a factory as a cigarette roller. She tells her sister's story, giving us a glimpse into their world:

> My sister is ten years old. Every morning at seven she goes to the bonded labor man, and every night at nine she comes home. He treats her badly; he hits her if he thinks she is working slowly or if she talks to the other children, he yells at her, he comes looking for her if she is sick and cannot go to work. I feel this is very difficult for her.
>
> I don't care about school or playing. I don't care about any of that. All I want is to bring my sister home from the bonded labor man. For 600 rupees* I can bring her home—that is our only chance to get her back.
>
> We don't have 600 rupees . . . we will never have 600 rupees.[1]
>
> * 600 rupees is the equivalent of approximately U.S. $17

These whom Christ thought of while dying on the cross must not be forgotten by His Body today. These for whom Christ suffered then must not be forsaken by us, His hands and feet, now. In the midst of advancing world evangelism, we cannot hold back the healing embrace with which to care and provide for these precious in the sight of God.

I'm particularly talking about the Dalits, or the "Untouchables"—the lowest caste of India. For 3,000 years, hundreds of millions of India's Untouchables have suffered oppression, slavery and countless atrocities in the name of religion. They are trapped in a caste system that denies them adequate education, safe drinking water, decent-paying jobs and the right to own land or a home. Segregated and oppressed, Dalits are frequently the victims of violent crime.

And just as the need is great, so is the possibility for Christ's power and love to be known.

In recent years, the door to these possibilities has been flung wide-open. Among Dalits and other low-caste groups that face similar repressive treatment, there has been a growing desire for freedom. Leaders representing approximately 700 million of these people have come forth demanding justice and freedom from caste slavery and persecution.

The turning point came on November 4, 2001, when tens of thousands of Dalits gathered for one of the most historic meetings of the 21st century, publicly declaring their desire to "quit Hinduism" and follow a faith of their own choosing.

Since that event, the Lord has led Gospel for Asia to tangibly express His love to Dalit, low-caste and tribal families in a unique way: *by reaching out to their children*.

GFA Bridge of Hope, our children's outreach program, is designed to rescue thousands of children in Asia from a life of poverty and hopelessness by giving them an education and introducing them to the love of God. Through this effort, churches are planted and entire communities are set on a course toward spiritual transformation as well as social development.

Today nearly 19,000 children are enrolled in 370 primary schools.[†] One of these schools is located in the village of native missionary and pastor Samuel Jagat.

When Samuel set out last year to establish a school for Dalit and low-caste families in his village, he had no idea that the group of 35 children attending would make such a remarkable difference in his ministry. But one little first-grade boy in his school was about to show him otherwise.

Nibun's mother had been ill with malaria for a long time. Doctors, priests and sorcerers could not find a cure, and her death seemed inevitable.

But Nibun had a little seed of hope in his heart—God's Word. Bible stories were a regular part of the curriculum at the village school, where teachers worked diligently to give children the best education while showing them the love of Christ. Like many other children, Nibun would come home and narrate

[†]As of October 2004

every story he had heard to his family.

One night, as Nibun and his family sat together beside his mother's bed, he told them how Jesus raised a widow's son from the dead. It became a turning point in all their lives.

"That night, after hearing this story," Nibun's father later shared, "I could not sleep. This story was burning in my heart again and again."

Nibun's father sought out Samuel the next morning. After hearing more about Jesus and His offer of salvation, the man asked the pastor to come and pray for his wife. "I believe Jesus will heal my wife just as he did the widow's son," he affirmed.

Nibun's mother, though weak in body, shared the same confidence: "My son talks about Jesus many times in our home. I believe Jesus will heal me."

Pastor Samuel laid hands on the dying woman and prayed for the Lord to raise her up; then he returned to his home.

The next day he saw Nibun and asked how his mother was doing.

"My mommy is walking around," he reported happily, "and this morning she prepared breakfast for us!"

When Samuel arrived at Nibun's house, he found a family transformed both physically and spiritually. They had all made a decision to follow Christ.

This openness to the Gospel among the Dalit people and other low-caste groups marks an unparalleled opportunity to reach some of the most unreached on earth today—up to 700 million souls. They are part of the harvest Jesus tells us is a vast field ready to be reaped and brought into God's eternal kingdom.

Bridge of Hope provides the means by which we can cross over to these millions and accomplish the task.

Nibun's father expresses it this way: "I thank God for this school and pray that He will use it to bring His light into many homes, just as He has done in our family."

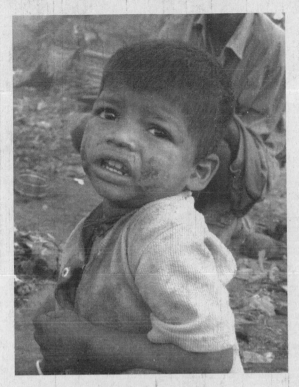

RIGHT: **FOR TOO MANY** Dalit children in India, the innocence of childhood is lost in poverty, child labor and exploitation. The problem of illiteracy—90 percent in some areas—leaves little room for hope.

BELOW: **EAGER TO LEARN** and full of spirit, Dalit children thrive at GFA Bridge of Hope schools like this one, where they get a good education and come to know that Jesus loves them.

ABOVE: **NARAYAN SHARMA** (far right) is director of Gospel for Asia's work in Nepal. Over the years, GFA has trained dedicated Nepali brothers and sisters, now winning the lost in some of the most difficult regions of this Hindu kingdom. White dots on the map represent churches they have planted.

BELOW: **OUR GOAL** is to establish local churches in unreached regions of Asia. This church is the fruit of one missionary's labors and was planted within his first year on the mission field. Depending upon the cost of land and its location, it takes an average of $10,000 to build a church that can seat 300 people.

RIGHT: THE MAJORITY OF YOUNG PEOPLE who attend GFA's Bible colleges come with a commitment to go to the most unreached areas to preach the Gospel. Gospel for Asia is committed to help these young people become firmly grounded in the Word of God before they are sent out.

BELOW: THEIR THREE-YEAR INTENSIVE TRAINING IS OVER, and now these young people are sent out to plant churches in completely unreached places. "If you are given the privilege to be a martyr for the Lord's sake," they are told, "remember that heaven is a much better place. He has promised never to leave or forsake you."

EVERY GFA BIBLE COLLEGE STUDENT learns the inductive Bible study method. Before graduation, students must successfully demonstrate their ability to study and communicate God's Word using this method. This ensures that as churches are planted, new believers will be firmly grounded in biblical truth.

GOSPEL FOR ASIA'S BURDEN is to train and equip 100,000 young people to go and plant churches among the unreached villages of the Indian subcontinent. Eighty percent of the graduates pictured here are on the mission field today, winning lost souls to Christ and establishing churches.

From the beginning of our ministry, we always used every opportunity to share the Gospel and see thousands come to Christ, especially in the most poor and needy communities. This has not changed. Since our beginning, we've had special ministries among leper colonies and slums, with dozens of churches having been planted among these needy people. So when we saw the desperate cry of help from the Dalits, we were eager to reach out to them.

The most tangible way we saw to do this was to set up primary schools for their children, as education often equals freedom in many of these nations.

In fact, one of the reasons so many children and their families stay enslaved as bond-laborers is for the simple fact that they cannot read the contract made between them and their loaner. Because of illiteracy, they are blindly taken advantage of and cheated out of not just money and time, but their futures.

Yet these schools are not just a social effort whose purpose and end is education. Not at all. For it is the love of Christ that constrains us to reach out in this way, knowing that each child and his family are precious in the sight of God.

These children and these schools are simply the bridge—the means by which to communicate the Gospel and see millions cross over from death to life.

Let me tell you an experience I had in the beginning stages of this potential ministry to the Dalits that changed my thinking and propelled us to move forward with the Bridge of Hope project.

It was while sleeping in the early hours of the morning that I had a dream. I was standing in front of a vast wheat field, looking out upon a harvest that was clearly ripe. I stood there for a while, overwhelmed at the size of the harvest. The field continued for what seemed like millions of endless acres for as far as the eye could see.

As I stood there watching the golden wheat sway in the breeze, I got this sudden understanding that I was looking out upon the harvest that Jesus spoke of in John 4 and Matthew 9. It was as though the Lord was telling me that this harvest is free for the taking, much as Psalm 2 tells us to ask for the nations and He will give them to us.

Overcome with excitement at seeing so much harvest ready for reaping and knowing that this represented millions upon millions of souls being rescued from an eternity in hell, I began to jump up and down. With all my might, I ran toward the field. But as I drew nearer, I was stopped. I couldn't go any farther. There was a wide, gaping river in between the harvest and myself, a river so deep and raging that I dared not step closer or try to cross. I had not seen it from where I stood before, but now I did.

My heart broke. I was only able to look at the harvest, unable to embrace it. I stood there weeping, feeling so helpless and full of despair.

All of a sudden there appeared before me a bridge reaching from one side of the vast river to the other. It was not a narrow bridge but was very broad and so huge.

As I watched, the bridge became completely filled with little children from all over Asia—poor, destitute Dalit children, like those I'd seen on the streets of Bombay, Calcutta, Dakar, Katmandu and other Asian cities.

Then it was as though someone spoke to me and said, "If you want to have this harvest, it's all yours. But this is the bridge that you must walk on to get it."

I woke up from my dream and realized that the Lord was speaking to me about something so significant: that if we follow His instruction, we will see these endless millions of Untouchables come to know Him. And the children would be the bridge to reach them.

I shared this dream with my colleagues, and we realized that God had given us this call to bring hope to the children of Asia. Through Bridge of Hope schools, children would be taught about the Lord Jesus Christ and experience His love, and through them, their communities and families would come to know the Lord.

Miraculously, this has been happening. God has been faithful to carry out the plans that He placed in our hearts.

In one part of India, we set up 50 schools among communities that previously did not welcome us or the Gospel message. As a matter of fact, when we first went into some of these communities to preach the Gospel, we were strongly opposed. But as our brothers went in to set up a primary school for the children, we were welcomed in a new light.

Within time, 50 Bridge of Hope schools were started in that region. Within 11 months' time, 37 churches were planted. And it all began with the little children learning about Jesus, going home and telling their parents; then miracle after miracle began to transpire! This is not an exception but something that we are seeing on a daily basis.

The Lord willing, as we move forward with a deep conviction to see the Gospel preached and the Great Commission truly fulfilled, we will see literally millions come to know the Lord. As we respond to their physical needs and do what we can in the name of Jesus, with the intention for them to hear the Good News of forgiveness from sin and redemption through the death and resurrection of the Lord Jesus Christ, communities will be changed, churches planted and disciples made.

The true fulfillment of the Great Commission must be at the heart of every endeavor that ministers to the felt needs of humanity. When this remains the element carrying the work forward, the love of Christ is shown in a tangible way that reaches down deep in the hearts of men and women, drawing them to the Savior of their souls.

When all is said and done, the bottom line must be "the poor have the gospel preached to them" (Matthew 11:5). If that is not done, we have failed.

Fourteen

The Need for Revolution

If we could spend only one minute in the flames and torment of hell, we would see how unloving the so-called gospel is that prevails in much of missions today.

Theology, which is only a fancy word for what we believe, makes all the difference on the mission field. When we go to the book of Acts, we find the disciples totally convinced about the lostness of man without Christ. Not even persecution could stop them from calling people everywhere to repent and turn to Christ.

Paul cries out in Romans 10:9–15 for the urgency of preaching Christ. In his day, the social and economic problems in cities like Corinth and Ephesus and other places were the same or worse than those we face today. Yet the apostles did not set out to establish social relief centers, hospitals or educational institutions. Paul declared in 1 Corinthians 2:1–2, "When I came to you, . . . I determined not to know any thing among you, save Jesus Christ, and him crucified."

Paul recognized that Jesus Christ was the ultimate answer to all man's problems. Although he was concerned about the poor saints, you cannot miss the primary emphasis of his life and message.

I have spoken in churches that had millions of dollars invested in buildings—churches with pastors known as excellent Bible teachers with a heart of love for people. Yet I have discovered that many of them have absolutely no missionary program of any kind.

In preaching to one of these churches, I made the following statement: "While you claim to be evangelicals and pour time and life into learning more and more biblical truths, in all honesty, I do not think you believe the Bible."

My listeners were shocked. But I continued.

"If you believed the Bible you say you believe, the very knowledge there is a real place called hell—where millions will go and spend eternity if they die without Christ—would make you the most desperate people in the world to give up everything you have to keep missions and reaching the lost as your top priority."

The problem with this congregation, as with many today, is that they did not believe in hell.

C.S. Lewis, that great British defender of the faith, wrote, "There is no doctrine which I would more willingly remove from Christianity than this [hell]. I would pay any price to be able to say truthfully, 'All will be saved.' "[1]

But Lewis, like us, realized that was neither truthful nor within his power to change.

Jesus Himself often spoke of hell and coming judgment. The Bible calls it the place of unquenchable fire, where the worms that eat the flesh don't die—a place of outer darkness where there is eternal weeping and gnashing of teeth. These and hundreds of other verses tell of a real place where lost men will spend eternity if they die without Jesus Christ.

Only a very few believers seem to have integrated the reality of hell into their lifestyle. In fact, it is difficult to feel that our friends who do not know Jesus really are destined to eternal hell.

Yet as I stressed in Chapter 12, many Christians hold within their hearts the idea that, somehow or other, ways of redemption are available to those who have not heard. The Bible does not give us a shred of hope for such a belief. It states clearly that it is "appointed unto men once to die, but after this the judgment" (Hebrews 9:27). There is no way out of death, hell, sin and the grave except Jesus Christ. He said, "I am the way, the truth, and the life: no man cometh unto the Father, but by me" (John 14:6).

How different our churches would be if we started to live by the true revelation of the Word of God about hell. Instead, local churches and missions, both in the West and in the East, have been infected with death and continue to pass out death to the millions of lost souls who surround us.

The Church Jesus called out of this world to be separated unto Himself has, to a great extent, forgotten her reason for existence. Her loss of balance is seen in the current absence of holiness, spiritual reality and concern for the lost. Substituted for the life she once knew are teaching and reaching for prosperity, pleasure, politics and social involvement.

"Evangelical Christianity," commented Tozer prophetically before his death, "is now tragically below the New Testament standard. Worldliness is an accepted fact of our way of life. Our religious mood is social instead of spiritual."

The further our leaders wander from the Lord, the more they turn to the ways of the world. One church in Dallas spent several million dollars to construct a gymnasium "to keep our young people interested in church." Many churches have become like secular clubs with softball teams, golf lessons, schools and exercise classes to keep people coming to their buildings and giving them their tithes. Some churches have gone so far from the Lord that they sponsor yoga and meditation courses—Western adaptations of Hindu religious exercises.

If this is what is considered mission outreach at home, is it any wonder the same churches fall prey to the seductive philosophy of Christian humanists when planning overseas missionary work?

Real Christian missions always is aware there is eternal hell to shun and heaven to gain. We need to restore the balanced vision General William Booth had when he started the Salvation Army. He had an unbelievable compassion for winning lost souls to Christ. His own words tell the story of what he envisioned for the movement: "Go for souls, and go for the worst."

What would Jesus do if He walked into our churches today?

I am afraid He would not be able to say to us: "You have kept the faith, you have run the race without turning left or right, and you have obeyed My command to reach this world." I believe He would go out to look for a whip, because we have made His Father's house a den of robbers. If that is so, then we must recognize that the hour is too desperate for us to continue to deceive ourselves. We are past the point of revival or reformation. If this Gospel is to be preached in all the world in our lifetime, we must have a Christian, heaven-sent revolution.

But before revolution can come, we must recognize the need for one. We are like a lost man looking at a road map. Before we can choose the right road that takes us to our destination, we must determine where we went wrong, go back to that point and start over. So my cry to the Body of Christ is simple: Turn back to the true Gospel road. We need to preach again the whole counsel of God. Our priority must again be placed on calling men to repentance and snatching them from hell-fire.

Time is short. If we are not willing to plead in prayer for a mission revolution—and let it start in our own personal lives, homes and churches—we will lose this generation to Satan.

We can go trading souls for bodies, or we can make a difference by sponsoring Bible-believing native missionaries overseas.

Several years ago, 40 Indian villages, once considered Christian, turned back to Hinduism. Could it be that whole villages that had experienced the liberating Gospel of Jesus Christ would turn back into the bondage of Satan?

No. These villages were called "Christian" only because they had been "converted" by missionaries who used hospitals, material goods and other incentives to attract them to Christianity. But when the material rewards were reduced—or when other competing movements offered similar benefits—these converts reverted to their old cultural ways. In missionary terms, they were "rice Christians."

When "rice" was offered, they changed their names and their religions, responding to the "rice." But they never understood the true Gospel of the Bible. After all the effort, these people were as lost as ever. But now they were even worse off—they were presented a completely wrong picture of what it means and what it takes to follow Christ.

Could that be what we fear in North America: no gyms—no softball teams—no converts?

The lesson from the mission field is that meeting physical needs alone does not get people to follow God. Whether hungry or full, rich or poor, human beings remain in rebellion against God without the power of the Gospel.

Unless we return to the biblical balance—to the Gospel of Jesus as He proclaimed it—we'll never be able to put the accent where it rightly belongs in the outreach mission of the Church.

Jesus was compassionate to human beings as total persons. He did all He could to help them, but He never forgot the main purpose of His earthly mission: to reconcile men to God, to die for sinners and redeem their souls from hell. Jesus cared for the spiritual side of man first, then the body.

This is illustrated clearly in Matthew 9:2–7 when He first forgave the sins of the paralytic, then healed his body.

In John 6:1–13, Jesus miraculously fed 5,000 hungry men plus women and children. He fed them after He preached, not before to attract their attention.

Later, in verse 26, we find that these people followed Jesus not because of His teachings or who He was, but because He had fed them. They even tried to make Him king for the wrong reason. Seeing the danger of their spiritual misunderstanding, Jesus withdrew from them. He didn't want fans but disciples.

The apostles did not fear to tell the beggar that "Silver and gold have I none; but such as I have give I thee . . . " (Acts 3:6). Then they preached the Gospel.

I have had similar experiences all across India. I have yet to meet a person who was not willing to hear the wonderful news of Jesus because of his or her physical condition.

As Christians, we must follow the example of Jesus. I do believe we must do all we can to relieve the pain and suffering around us. We must love our neighbors as ourselves in all areas of life. But we must keep supreme the priority of sharing the message of salvation with them—and we must never minister to the physical needs at the expense of preaching Christ. This is biblical balance, the true Gospel of Jesus.

Fifteen

The Real Culprit: Spiritual Darkness

My hosts in the southern U.S. city where I was preaching at a mission conference had thoughtfully booked me into a motel room. It was good to have a few minutes alone, and I looked forward to having some time for prayer and Scripture meditation.

While settling in, I flipped on the big TV set that dominated the room. What burst on the screen shocked me more than anything I had ever seen in America. There in beautiful color was an attractive woman seated in the lotus position teaching yoga. I watched in horror and amazement as she praised the health benefits of the breathing techniques and other exercises of this Eastern religious practice. What her viewers did not know is that yoga is designed for one purpose only—to open up the mind and body to receive visitations from demon spirits.

Because this American yogi was dressed in a body suit, claimed a Ph.D. degree and was on educational TV, I assume many of the viewers were deceived into believing this was just another harmless exercise show. But those of us born and raised in nations dominated by the power of darkness know that hundreds of Eastern religions are marketing themselves in the United States and Canada under innocuous—even scientific-sounding—brand names.

Few Westerners, when they see news reports of the poverty,

suffering and violence in Asia, take time to stop and ask why the East is bound into an endless cycle of suffering while Western nations are so blessed.

Secular humanists are quick to reel out many historic and pseudoscientific reasons for the disparity, because they are unwilling to face the truth. But the real reason is simple: The Judeo-Christian heritage of Europe has brought the favor of God, while false religions have brought the curse of Babylon on all the nations of Asia.

Mature Christians realize the Bible teaches there are only two religions in this world. There is the worship of the one true God, and there is a false system of demonic alternative invented in ancient Persia. From there, Persian armies and priests spread their faith to India where it took root. Hindu missionaries in turn spread it throughout the rest of Asia. Animism, Buddhism and all other Asian religions have a common heritage in this one religious system.

Because many Westerners are unaware of this fact, demonic influences now are able to spread Eastern mysticism in the West through pop culture, rock bands, singers and even university professors. The media have become the new vehicle for the spread of demon worship and idolatry by American gurus.

It is hard to blame average Christians for misunderstanding what is happening to them and the Judeo-Christian heritage that has brought such blessings on their land. Most have never taken the time to study and discern the real situation in the Orient. Few pastors or prophets are sounding the alarm.

In Asia, the religion of Babylon is woven into every waking minute of the day. Without Christ, people live to serve demon spirits. Religion relates to everything, including your name, birth, education, marriage, business deals, contracts, travel and death.

Because Oriental culture and religion are a mystery, many

people in the West are fascinated by it without knowing the power of these demons to blind and enslave their followers. What routinely follows the mystery religions of Babylon are degradation, humiliation, poverty and suffering—even death.

Most believers in America, I find, are overwhelmed by the TV and media news reports from Asia. The numbers reported are beyond imagination, and the injustice, poverty, suffering and violence appear to be unstoppable. All things Oriental appear to be mysterious, and measured either on a grand scale or by one so different that it cannot be compared to things familiar.

In all my travels, therefore, I have found it is extremely difficult for most people to relate to Asia's needs. Sometimes I wish I could just scoop up my audience and take them on a six-month tour of Asia. But because that is not possible, I must use words, pictures, slides and video films to paint a clearer picture. Since nearly two out of every three people in the world live there—more than the combined populations of Europe, Africa, North America and South America, it is important that we take the time to understand the real need.

From the standpoint of Christian missions, these are more than just big numbers. Asia makes up the vast majority of the more than 2 billion hidden people who are being missed by traditional missionary efforts and mass media evangelism. They are the most lost of the lost—trapped in utter spiritual darkness.

What are the challenges facing native missions today? How real are the needs? How can Christians best help the Asian Church and its missionary efforts?

I am not trying to minimize the social and material needs of the Asian nations, but it is important to reemphasize that Asia's basic problem is a spiritual one. When the Western media focus almost entirely on our problems of hunger, for example showing all these pictures of starving children on TV, it is difficult for Americans not to get the false impression that hunger is the biggest problem.

But what causes the hunger? Asian Christians know these horrible conditions are only symptoms of the real problem—spiritual bondage to satanic philosophies. The key factor—and the most neglected—in understanding India's hunger problem is the Hindu belief system and its effect on food production. Most people know of the "sacred cows" that roam free, eating tons of grain while nearby people starve. But a lesser-known and more sinister culprit is another animal protected by religious belief—the rat.

According to those who believe in reincarnation, the rat must be protected as a likely recipient for a reincarnated soul on its way up the ladder of spiritual evolution to Nirvana. Though many reject this and seek to poison rats, large-scale efforts of extermination have been thwarted by religious outcry. As one of India's statesmen has said, "India's problems will never cease until her religion changes."

Rats eat or spoil 20 percent of India's food grain every year. A recent survey in the wheat-growing district of Hapur in North India revealed an average of 10 rats per house.

Of one harvest of cereals in India, including maize, wheat, rice, millet and so on—a total of 134 million metric tons—the 20 percent loss from rats amounted to 26.8 million metric tons. The picture becomes more comprehensible by imagining a train of boxcars carrying that amount of grain. With each car holding about 82 metric tons, the train would contain 327,000 cars and stretch for 3,097 miles. The annual food grain loss in India would fill a train longer than the distance between New York and Los Angeles.

The devastating effects of the rat in India should make it an object of scorn. Instead, because of the spiritual blindness of the people, the rat is protected and in some places, like a temple 30 miles south of Bikaner in North India, even worshiped.

According to an article in the *India Express*, "Hundreds of rats, called 'kabas' by the devotees, scurry around merrily in the large compound of the temple and sometimes even around the image of the goddess Karni Devi situated in a cave. The rats are fed on prasad offered by the devotee or by the temple management. Legend has it that the fortunes of the community are linked to that of the rats.

"One has to walk cautiously through the temple compound; for if a rat is crushed to death, it is not only considered a bad omen but may also invite severe punishment. One is considered lucky if a rat climbs over one's shoulder. Better still to see a white rat."

Clearly, the agony we see in the faces of those starving children and beggars is actually caused by centuries of religious slavery. In my own beloved homeland of India, thousands of lives and billions of dollars go into social programs, education and medical and relief efforts every year. Many of the crisis problems that are considered disasters in the United States would only be normal, everyday living conditions in most of Asia. When we have disasters in the Orient, the death tolls read like Vietnam War body counts. Asian governments struggle with these tremendous social problems and limited resources.

Yet despite all these massive social programs, the problems of hunger, population and poverty continue to grow. The real culprit is not a person, lack of natural resources or a system of government. It is spiritual darkness. It thwarts every effort to make progress. It dooms our people to misery—both in this world and in the world to come. The single most important social reform that can be brought to Asia is the Gospel of Jesus Christ. More than 400 million of my people have never heard the name of Jesus Christ. They need the hope and truth that only the Lord Jesus can provide.

Recently, for instance, one native missionary, who serves the Lord in Jammu, asked a shopkeeper at the market if he knew Jesus. After thinking a moment, he said, "Sir, I know everyone in our village. There is not one by that name who lives here. Why don't you go to the next village? He may live there."

Frequently native missionary evangelists find people who ask if Jesus is the brand name of a new soap or patent medicine.

In fact, in India proper there are more than 1 billion people—four times the population of the United States. Only 2.4 percent of these call themselves Christians.[1] Although this figure reflects the official government census, other Christian sources believe the number to be as high as 7.4 percent.[2] Still, India, with nearly 500,000 unevangelized villages, is undoubtedly one of the greatest evangelistic challenges facing the world Christian community today. If present trends continue, it will soon be the world's most populous nation. Many of India's 29 states have larger populations than whole nations in Europe and other parts of the world.

Not only are their populations huge, but each state is usually as distinctive as if it were another world. Most have completely different cultures, dress, diet and languages. But few nations in Asia are homogeneous. Most are like India to some extent, nations that are patchwork quilts of many languages, peoples and tribes. This diversity, in fact, is what makes Asia such a tremendous challenge to missionary work.

Sixteen

Enemies of the Cross

The native missionary movement, the only hope for these unreached nations, is not going unchallenged by either Satan or the world. Revivals of traditional religions such as Islam and Hinduism, the growth of secular materialism including communism, and the traditional cultural and nationalist barriers are all united in opposition to Christian mission activity.

"I was brought up in a home where we worshiped many gods," says Masih, who for years sought spiritual peace through self-discipline, yoga and meditation as required by his caste. "I even became the priest in our village, but I couldn't find the peace and joy I wanted.

"One day I received a Gospel tract and read about the love of Jesus Christ. I answered the offer on the leaflet and enrolled in a correspondence course to learn more about Jesus. On January 1, 1978, I gave my life to Jesus Christ. I was baptized three months later and took the Christian name 'Masih,' which means 'Christ.'"

In Asia, baptism and the taking of a Christian name symbolize a complete break with the pagan past. To avoid the censure, which often comes with baptism, some wait years before they are baptized. But Masih didn't wait. The reaction was swift.

When his parents realized their son had rejected their gods, they began a campaign of persecution. To escape, Masih went to Kota in Rajasthan to search for a job. For six months he worked in a factory and meanwhile joined a local group of believers. Through their encouragement, he enrolled in a Bible institute and began to master the Scriptures.

During his three years of study, he made his first trip home. "My father sent a telegram asking me to come home," Masih recalls. "He said he was 'terribly ill.' When I arrived, my family and friends asked me to renounce Christ. When I didn't, much persecution followed, and my life was in danger. I had to flee."

Returning to school, Masih thought God would lead him to minister to some other part of India. He was shocked at the answer to his prayers.

"As I waited on the Lord, He guided me to go back and work among my own people," he says. "He wanted me to share the love of God through Christ with them, like the healed demoniac of Gadara whom He sent back to his own village."

Today, Ramkumar Masih—a former priest—is involved in church planting in his home city and surrounding villages, working among both Hindus and Muslims in a basically hostile environment.

Although Masih has not had to pay the ultimate price to win his people to Christ, every year a number of Christian missionaries and ordinary believers are killed for their faith throughout Asia. The total in the past century is estimated at 45 million, undoubtedly more than the total killed during the preceding 19 centuries of Church history.[1]

What are these enemies of the cross that seek to oppose the advance of the Gospel in the nations that need so much to hear of its hope and salvation? They are nothing new—just reawakened devices of the enemy, some of his final ploys to keep these nations bound.

Traditional Religions

Revivals of traditional religions are occurring all over Asia. Although few countries have gone the route of Iran—where a religious revival of Islam actually toppled the state—religious factionalism is a major problem in many countries.

When government, media and educational institutions are taken over by atheistic materialists, most nations experience a great backlash. As traditional religious leaders are finding out, it is not enough to drive Western nations out. Secular humanists are in firm control of most Asian governments, and many traditional religious leaders miss the power they once exercised.

At the grassroots level, traditional religion and nationalism often are deliberately confused and exploited by political leaders for short-term gain. In the villages, traditional religions still have a powerful hold on the minds of most people. Almost every village or community has a favorite idol or deity—there are 330 million gods in the Hindu pantheon alone. In addition, various animistic cults, which involve the worship of powerful spirits, are openly practiced alongside Islam, Hinduism and Buddhism.

In many areas, the village temple still is the center of informal education, tourism and civic pride. Religion is big business, and temples take in vast sums of money annually. Millions of priests and amateur practitioners of the occult arts also are profiteering from the continuation and expansion of traditional religions. Like the silversmiths in Ephesus, they aren't taking the spread of Christianity lightly. Religion, nationalism and economic gain mix as a volatile explosive that Satan uses to blind the eyes of millions.

But God is calling native missionaries to preach the Gospel anyway, and many are taking the Good News into areas solidly controlled by traditional religions.

The Spirit of the Antichrist

But the enemies of the cross include more than just traditional religionists. A new force, even more powerful, is now sweeping across Asia. It is what the Bible calls the spirit of the Antichrist—the new religion of secular materialism. Often manifested as some form of communism, it has taken control of governments in a number of states, including Myanmar, Cambodia, China, Laos, North Korea and Vietnam. But even in those Asian nations with democracies like India and Japan, it has gained some control of the state in various noncommunist forms.

The temples of this new religion are atomic reactors, oil refineries, hospitals and shopping malls. The priests are most often the technicians, scientists and military generals who are impatiently striving to rebuild the nations of Asia in the image of the industrial West. The shift of political power in most of Asia has gone toward these men and women who promise health, peace and prosperity without a supernatural god—for man himself is their god.

In one sense, secular humanism and materialism correctly diagnose traditional religion as a major source of oppression and poverty throughout Asia. Humanism is a natural enemy of theistic religion because it is a worldly and scientific method to solve the problems of mankind without God. As a result of this growing, scientific materialism, strong secularistic movements exist in every Asian nation. They unite and seek to eliminate the influence of all religion—including Christianity—from society. Modern Asia, in the great cities and capitals where secular humanism reigns supreme, is controlled by many of the same drives and desires that have dominated the West for the past 100 years.

The Anti-Christian Pressure of the World—the Culture

If traditional Asian religions represent an attack of the devil on Christianity, then secular humanism is an attack of the flesh.

That leaves only one enemy to discuss, the anti-Christian pressure of the world. This final barrier to Christ, and still probably the strongest of all, is the culture itself.

When Mahatma Gandhi returned to India from years of living in England and South Africa, he quickly realized the "Quit India" movement was failing because its national leadership was not willing to give up European ways. So even though he was Indian, he had to renounce his Western dress and customs or he would not have been able to lead his people out from under the British yoke. He spent the rest of his life relearning how to become an Indian again—in dress, food, culture and lifestyle. Eventually he gained acceptance by the common people of India. The rest is history. He became the father of my nation, the George Washington of modern India.

The same principle holds true of evangelistic and church-planting efforts in all of Asia. We must learn to adapt to the culture. This is why the native evangelist, who comes from the native soil, is so effective. When Americans here in the United States are approached by yellow-robed Krishna worshipers—with their shaved heads and prayer beads—they reject Hinduism immediately. In the same way, Hindus reject Christianity when it comes in Western forms.

Have Asians rejected Christ? Not really. In most cases they have rejected only the trappings of Western culture that have fastened themselves onto the Gospel. This is what the apostle Paul was referring to when he said he was willing to become "all things to all men" in order that he might win some.

When Asians share Christ with other Asians in a culturally acceptable way, the results are startling. One native missionary we support in northwest India, Jager, now has evangelized 60 villages and established 30 churches in a difficult area of Punjab. He has led hundreds to Christ. On one trip to India, I went out of my way to visit Jager and his wife. I had to see for myself what kind of program he was using.

Imagine my surprise when I found Jager was not using any special technology at all—unless you want to call the motor scooter and tracts that we supplied "technology." He was living just like the people. He had only a one-room house made of dung and mud. The kitchen was outside, also made of mud—the same stuff with which everything else is constructed in that region. To cook the food, his wife squatted in front of an open fire just like the neighboring women. What was so remarkable about this brother was that everything about him and his wife was so truly Indian. There was absolutely nothing foreign.

I asked Jager what kept him going in the midst of such incredible challenge and suffering. He said, "Waiting upon the Lord, my brother." I discovered he spent two to three hours daily in prayer, reading and meditating on the Bible. This is what it takes to win Asia for Christ. This is the kind of missionary for which our nations cry out.

Jager was won to Christ by another native evangelist, who explained the living God to Jager while he was still a devout Hindu. He told of a God who hates sin and became a man to die for sinners and set them free. This was the first time the Gospel ever was preached in his village, and Jager followed the man around for several days.

Finally, he received Jesus as his Lord and was disowned by his family. Overjoyed and surprised by his newfound life, he went about distributing tracts from village to village, telling about Jesus. In the end, he sold his two shops. With the money he earned, he conducted evangelistic meetings in local villages.

This is a man of the culture, bringing Christ to his own people in culturally acceptable ways. The support we Asians need from the West, if we are to complete the work Christ has left us, must go to recruit, equip and send out an army of native missionary evangelists.

Native evangelists are prepared to meet the three big challenges we are now facing in the Orient.

One, they often understand the culture, customs and lifestyle as well as the language. They do not have to spend valuable time in lengthy preparations.

Two, the most effective communication occurs between peers. Although there still may be social barriers to overcome, they are much smaller and more easily identified.

Three, it is a wise investment of our resources because the native missionary works more economically than foreigners can.

One of the most basic laws of creation is that every living thing reproduces after its own kind. This fact applies in evangelism and discipleship, just as it does in other areas. If we are going to see a mass people movement to Christ, it will be done only through fielding many more thousands of native missionaries.

How many are needed? In India alone we still have 500,000 villages to reach. Looking at other nations, we realize thousands more remain without a witness. If we are to reach all the other hamlets open to us right now, Gospel for Asia will need additional native missionary evangelists by the tens of thousands. The cost to support this army will run into the millions annually. But this is only a fraction of the $94 billion that the North American Church lavished on other needs and desires in 2000.[2] And the result will be a revolution of love that will bring millions of Asians to Christ.

So, are native missionaries prepared to carry on cross-cultural evangelism? The answer is yes, and with great effectiveness! Most of the native missionaries we support, in fact, are involved in some form of cross-cultural evangelism. Often, GFA evangelists find they must learn a new language, plus adopt different dress and dietary customs. However, because the cultures are frequently neighbors or share a similar heritage, the transition is much easier than it would be for someone coming from the West.

Even though my homeland has 18 major languages and 1,650 dialects[3]—each representing a different culture—it is still relatively easy for an Indian to make a transition from one culture to another. In fact, almost anyone in Pakistan, India, Bangladesh, Myanmar, Nepal, Bhutan, Thailand and Sri Lanka can relatively quickly cross-minister in a neighboring culture.

Native workers who seek to learn new languages and plant churches in other cultures face special challenges. In this particular endeavor, Gospel for Asia seeks to work with like-minded agencies that can help the native worker overcome these challenges.

The challenge of Asia cries out to us. The enemies of the cross abound, but none of them can stand against us as we move out in the authority and power of the Lord Jesus. The problems we face are indeed great, but they can be overcome through tens of thousands of native missionary evangelists.

Seventeen

The Water of Life in a Foreign Cup

When we think about the awesome challenge of Asia, it is not too much to ask for a new army of missionaries to reach these nations for Christ. And tens of thousands of native missionaries are being raised up by the Lord in all these Two-Thirds World nations right now. They are Asians, many of whom already live in the nation they must reach or in nearby cultures just a few hundred miles from the unevangelized villages to which they will be sent by the Lord.

The situation in world missions is depressing only when you think of it in terms of 19th-century Western colonialism. If the actual task of world evangelization depends on the "sending of the white missionary," obeying the Great Commission truly becomes more impossible every day. But, praise God, the native missionary movement is growing, ready today to complete the task.

The primary message I have for every Christian, pastor and mission leader is that we are witnessing a new day in missions. Just a few short years ago, no one dreamed the Asian Church would be ready to lead the final thrust. But dedicated native evangelists are beginning to go out and reach their own.

Even more exciting: You have a role. God is calling all of us to be part of what He is doing.

We can make it possible for millions of brown and yellow

feet to move out with the liberating Gospel of Jesus. With the prayer and financial support of the Western Church, they can preach the Word to the lost multitudes. The whole family of God is needed. Thousands of native missionaries will go to the lost if Christians in the West will help by sharing resources with them.

This is why I believe God called me to the United States. The only reason I stay here is to help serve our Asian brethren by bringing their needs before God's people in the West. A whole new generation of Christians needs to know that this profound shift in the mission task has taken place. North American believers need to know they are needed as "senders" to pray and to help the native brothers go.

The waters of missions have been muddied. Today many Christians are unable to think clearly about the real issues because Satan has sent a deceiving spirit to blind their eyes. I do not make this statement lightly. Satan knows that to stop world evangelism he must confuse the minds of Western Christians. This he has done quite effectively. The facts speak for themselves.

The average North American Christian gives only 50 cents a week to global missions.[1] Imagine what that means. Missions is the primary task of the Church, our Lord's final command to us before His ascension. Jesus died on the cross to start a missionary movement. He came to show God's love, and we are left here to continue that mission. Yet this most important task of the Church is receiving less than one percent of all our finances.

Remember, of the Western missionaries who are sent overseas, many are involved in efforts of social work in the Two-Thirds World and not in the primary task of preaching the Gospel and planting churches.

And approximately 85 percent of all missionary finances are

being used by Western missionaries who are working among the established churches on the field—not for pioneer evangelism to the lost.[2]

Consequently, most of that 50 cents a week the average American Christian has given to missions actually was spent on projects or programs other than proclaiming the Gospel of Christ.

But a shift has taken place in the past six decades or so. At the end of World War II, almost the entire work of the Great Commission was being done by a handful of white foreigners. To these Christian mission leaders, it was impossible to even imagine reaching all the thousands of distinct cultural groups in the colonies. So they focused their attention on the major cultural groups in easy-to-reach centers of trade and government.

In most of the Asian nations, nearly 200 years of mission work had been accomplished under the watchful gaze of colonial governors when the era finally ended in 1945. During that time, Western missionaries appeared to be a vital part of the fabric of Western colonial government. Even the few churches that were established among the dominant cultural groups appeared weak. Like the local government and economy, they too were directly controlled by foreigners. Few were indigenous or independent of Western missionaries. Not surprisingly, the masses shunned these strange centers of alien religion, much as most Americans avoid "Krishna missions" in the United States today.

In this atmosphere, the thought of going beyond the major cultural groups—reaching out to the unfinished task—was naturally put off. Those masses of people in rural areas, ethnic subcultures, tribal groups and minorities would have to wait. Teaching them was still generations away—unless, of course, more white foreign missionaries could be recruited to go to them.

153

But this was not to be. When the colonial-era missionaries returned to take control of "their" churches, hospitals and schools, they found the political climate had changed radically. They met a new hostility from Asian governments. Something radical had happened during World War II. The nationalists had organized and were on the march.

Soon political revolution was sweeping the Two-Thirds World. With the independence of one nation after another, the missionaries lost their positions of power and privilege. In the 25 years following World War II, 71 nations broke free of Western domination. And with their new freedom, most decided Western missionaries would be among the first symbols of the West to go. Now 86 nations—with more than half of the world's population—forbid or seriously restrict foreign missionaries.[3]

But there is a bright side to the story. The effect of all this on the emerging churches of Asia has been electric. Far from slowing the spread of the Gospel, the withdrawal of foreign missionaries has freed the Gospel from the Western traditions that foreign missionaries had unwittingly added to it.

Sadhu Sundar Singh, a pioneer native missionary evangelist, used to tell a story that illustrates the importance of presenting the Gospel in culturally acceptable terms.

A high-caste Hindu, he said, had fainted one day from the summer heat while sitting on a train in a railway station. A train employee ran to a water faucet, filled a cup with water and brought it to the man in an attempt to revive him. But in spite of his condition, the Hindu refused. He would rather die than accept water in the cup of someone from another caste.

Then someone else noticed that the high-caste passenger had left his own cup on the seat beside him. So he grabbed it, filled it with water and returned to offer it to the panting heat victim who immediately accepted the water with gratitude.

Then Sundar Singh would say to his hearers, "This is what I have been trying to say to missionaries from abroad. You have been offering the water of life to the people of India in a foreign cup, and we have been slow to receive it. If you will offer it in our own cup in an indigenous form then we are much more likely to accept it."

Today, a whole new generation of Spirit-led young native leaders is mapping strategies to complete the evangelization of our Asian homelands. In almost every country of Asia, I personally know local missionaries who are effectively winning their people to Christ using culturally acceptable methods and styles.

Although persecution in one form or another still exists in most Asian nations, the postcolonial national governments have guaranteed almost unlimited freedom to native missionaries. Just because Westerners have been forbidden, the expansion of the Church does not have to cease.

For some diabolical reason, news of this dramatic change has not reached the ears of most believers in our churches. While God by His Holy Spirit has been raising up a new army of missionaries to carry on the work of the Great Commission, most North American believers have sat unmoved. This, I have discovered, is not because Christians here are lacking in generosity. When they are told the need, they respond quickly. They are not involved only because they do not know the real truth about what is happening in Asia today.

I believe we are being called to be involved by sharing prayerfully and financially in the great work that lies ahead. As we do this, perhaps we will see together the fulfillment of that awesome prophecy in Revelation 7:9–10:

And, lo, a great multitude, which no man could number, of all nations, and kindreds, and people, and tongues, stood before the throne, and before the Lamb, clothed with white robes, and palms in their hands; And cried with a loud voice, saying, Salvation to our God which sitteth upon the throne, and unto the Lamb.

This prediction is about to come true. Now, for the first time in history, we can see the final thrust taking place as God's people everywhere unite to make it possible.

What should intrigue us—especially here in the West—is the way the native missionary movement is flourishing without the help and genius of our Western planning. The Holy Spirit, when we give Him the freedom to work, prompts spontaneous growth and expansion. Until we recognize the native missionary movement as the plan of God for this period in history and until we are willing to become servants to what He is doing, we are in danger of frustrating the will of God.

Eighteen

A Global Vision

Should all Western missionaries pull out of Asia forever? Of course not. God still sovereignly calls Western missionaries to do unique and special tasks in Asia. But we must understand that when it comes to in which Western missionaries are no longer able to do church planting as past eras allowed, the priority must then be to support efforts of indigenous mission works through financial aid and intercessory prayer.

As gently as I can, I have to say to North Americans that anti-American prejudice is still running high in most of Asia. In fact, this is a section I write with the greatest fear and trembling—but these truths must be said if we are to accomplish the will of God in the Asian mission fields today.

"There are times in history," writes Dennis E. Clark in *The Third World and Mission,* "when however gifted a person may be, he can no longer effectively proclaim the Gospel to those of another culture. A German could not have done so in Britain in 1941 nor could an Indian in Pakistan during the war of 1967, and it will be extremely difficult for Americans to do so in the Third World of the 1980s and 1990s."[1] This is much more true—and the situation is even worse—today.

For the sake of Christ—because the love of Jesus constrains us—we need to review the financial and mission policies of our churches and North American missionary-sending agencies.

Every believer should reconsider his or her own stewardship practices and submit to the Holy Spirit's guidance in how best to support the global outreach of the Church.

I am not calling for an end to denominational mission programs or the closing down of the many hundreds of missions here in North America—but I am asking us to reconsider the missionary policies and practices that have guided us for the past 200 years. It is time to make some basic changes and launch the biggest missionary movement in history—one that primarily helps send forth native missionary evangelists rather than Western staff.

The principle I argue for is this: We believe the most effective way now to win Asia for Christ is through prayer and financial support for the native missionary force that God is raising up in the Two-Thirds World. As a general rule, for the following reasons I believe it is wiser to support native missionaries in their own lands than to send Western missionaries.

One, it is wise stewardship. According to Bob Granholm, former executive director of Frontiers in Canada, it costs between $25,000 to $30,000 per year to support a missionary on the mission field. Although this may be true for ministries like Frontiers, Operation Mobilization, Youth With A Mission and a few other organizations, in my research with more traditional agencies, the cost may be much higher. One mission organization estimates it costs around $80,000 per year to keep a missionary couple in India.[2] With even a modest inflation rate of three percent, this cost will exceed $100,000 in less than 10 years.

During a recent consultation on world evangelism, Western missionary leaders called for 200,000 new missionaries by the year 2000 in order to keep pace with their estimates of population growth. The cost of even that modest missionary force would be a staggering $20 billion a year. When you realize that in 2000 North American Christians contributed just $5.5 billion for missions,[3] we are facing an astronomical fund-raising effort. There has to be an alternative.

In India, for only the cost of flying an American from New York to Bombay, a native missionary already on the field can minister for years! Unless we take these facts into account, we will lose the opportunity of our age to reach untold millions with the Gospel. Today it is outrageously extravagant to send North American missionaries overseas unless there are compelling reasons to do so. From a strictly financial standpoint, sending American missionaries overseas is one of the worst investments we can make today.

Two, in many places the presence of Western missionaries perpetuates the myth that Christianity is the religion of the West. Bob Granholm states, "While the current internationalization of the missionary task force is a very encouraging development, it is often wiser to not have a western face on the efforts to extend the Kingdom."

Roland Allen says it better than I in his classic book *The Spontaneous Expansion of the Church:*

> Even if the supply of men and funds from Western sources was unlimited and we could cover the whole globe with an army of millions of foreign missionaries and establish stations thickly all over the world, the method would speedily reveal its weakness, as it is already beginning to reveal it.
>
> The mere fact that Christianity was propagated by such an army, established in foreign stations all over the world, would inevitably alienate the native populations, who would see in it the growth of the denomination of a foreign people. They would see themselves robbed of their religious independence, and would more and more fear the loss of their social independence.
>
> Foreigners can never successfully direct the propagation of any faith throughout a whole country. If the faith does not

become naturalized and expand among the people by its own vital power, it exercises an alarming and hateful influence, and men fear and shun it as something alien. It is then obvious that no sound missionary policy can be based upon multiplication of missionaries and mission stations. A thousand would not suffice; a dozen might be too many.[4]

A friend of mine who heads a missionary organization similar to ours recently told me the story of a conversation he had with some African church leaders.

"We want to evangelize our people," they said, "but we can't do it so long as the white missionaries remain. Our people won't listen to us. The communists and the Muslims tell them all white missionaries are spies sent out by their governments as agents for the capitalistic imperialists. We know it isn't true, but newspaper reports tell of how some missionaries are getting funds from the CIA. We love the American missionaries in the Lord. We wish they could stay, but the only hope for us to evangelize our own country is for all white missionaries to leave."

Untold millions of dollars still are being wasted today by our denominations and missions as they erect and protect elaborate organizational frameworks overseas. There was a time when Western missionaries needed to go into these countries in which the Gospel was not preached. But now a new era has begun, and it is important that we officially acknowledge this. God has raised up indigenous leaders who are more capable than outsiders to finish the job.

Now we must send the major portion of our funds to native missionaries and church growth movements. But this does not mean we do not appreciate the legacy left to us from Western missionaries. Although I believe changes must be made in our missionary methods, we praise God for the tremendous contribution Western missionaries have made in many Two-Thirds World countries where Christ was never before preached.

Through their faithfulness, many were won to Jesus, churches were started and the Scriptures were translated. These converts are today's native missionaries.

Silas Fox, a Canadian who served in South India, learned to speak the local native language of Telugu and preached the Word with such anointing that hundreds of present-day Christian leaders in Andhra Pradesh can trace their spiritual beginnings to his ministry.

I thank God for missionaries like Hudson Taylor, who against all wishes of his foreign mission board became a Chinese in his lifestyle and won many to Christ. I am not worthy to wipe the dust from the feet of thousands of faithful men and women of our Lord who went overseas during times like these.

Jesus set the example for native missionary work. "As my Father hath sent me," He said, "even so send I you" (John 20:21). The Lord became one of us in order to win us to the love of God. He knew He could not be an alien from outer space so He became incarnated into our bodies.

For any missionary to be successful he must identify with the people he plans to reach. Because Westerners usually cannot do this, they are ineffective. Anyone—Asian or American—who insists on still going out as a representative of Western missions and organizations will be ineffective today. We cannot maintain a Western lifestyle or outlook and work among the poor of Asia.

Three, Western missionaries, and the money they bring, compromise the natural growth and independence of the national Church. The economic power of the North American dollar distorts the picture as North American missionaries hire key national leaders to run their organizations.

Recently I met with a missionary executive of one of the major U.S. denominations. He is a loving man whom I deeply respect as a brother in Christ, but he heads the colonial-style extension of his denomination into Asia.

We talked about mutual friends and the exciting growth that is occurring in the national churches of India. We shared much in the Lord. I quickly found he had as much respect as I did for the Indian brothers God is choosing to use in India today. Yet he would not support these men who are so obviously anointed by God.

I asked him why. His denomination is spending millions of dollars annually to open up their churches in Asia—money I felt could be far better used supporting native missionaries in the churches the Holy Spirit is spontaneously birthing.

His answer shocked and saddened me.

"Our policy," he admitted without shame, "is to use the nationals only to expand churches with our denominational distinctives."

The words rolled around in my mind, "use the nationals." This is what colonialism was all about, and it is still what the neocolonialism of most Western missions is all about. With their money and technology, many organizations are simply buying people to perpetuate their foreign denominations, ways and beliefs.

In Thailand, a group of native missionaries was "bought away" by a powerful American parachurch organization. Once effectively winning their own people to Christ and planting churches in the Thai way, their leaders were given scholarships to train in the United States. The American organization provided them with expense accounts, vehicles and posh offices in Bangkok.

What price did the native missionary leader pay? He must use foreign literature, films and the standard method of this highly technical American organization. No consideration is being made of how effective these tools and methods will be in building the Thai Church. They will be used whether they are effective or not because they are written into the training manuals and handbooks of this organization.

After all, the reasoning of this group goes, these programs worked in Los Angeles and Dallas—they must work in Thailand as well!

This kind of thinking is the worst neocolonialism. To use God-given money to hire people to perpetuate our ways and theories is a modern method of old-fashioned imperialism. No method could be more unbiblical.

The sad fact is this: God already was doing a wonderful work in Thailand by His Holy Spirit in a culturally acceptable way. Why didn't this American group have the humility to bow before the Holy Spirit and say, "Have Thine own way, Lord"? If they wanted to help, I think the best way would have been to support what God already was doing by His Holy Spirit. By the time this group finds out what a mistake it has made, the missionaries who messed up the local church will be going home for furlough—probably never to return.

At their rallies they will tell stories of victories in Thailand as they evangelized the country American-style; but no one will be asking the most important question, "Where is the fruit that remains?"

Often we become so preoccupied with expanding our own organizations that we do not comprehend the great sweep of the Holy Spirit of God as He has moved upon the peoples of the world. Intent upon building "our" churches, we have failed to see how Christ is building "His" Church in every nation. We must stop looking at the lost world through the eyes of our particular denomination. Then we will be able to win the lost souls to Jesus instead of trying to add more numbers to our man-made organizations to please the headquarters that control the funds.

Four, Western missionaries cannot easily go to the countries where most so-called "hidden people" live. More than 2 billion of these people exist in our world today. Millions upon millions of lost souls have never heard the Gospel. We hear many cries that we should go to them, but who will go? The hidden people almost all live in countries closed or severely restricted to American and European missionaries.

Of the more than 135,000 North American missionaries now actively commissioned, fewer than 10,000 are working among totally unreached peoples.[5] The vast majority are working among the existing churches or where the Gospel already is preached.

Although more than one-third of the countries in the world today forbid the Western missionary, now the native missionary can go to the nearest hidden people group. For example, an Indian can go to Nepal with the Gospel much easier than anyone from the West.

Five, Western missionaries seldom are effective today in reaching Asians and establishing local churches in the villages of Asia. Unlike the Western missionary, the native missionary can preach, teach and evangelize without being blocked by most of the barriers that confront Westerners. As a native of the country or region, he knows the cultural taboos instinctively. Frequently, he already has mastered the language or a related dialect. He moves freely and is accepted in good times and bad as one who belongs. He does not have to be transported thousands of miles nor does he require special training and language schools.

I remember an incident—one of many—that illustrates this sad fact. During my days of preaching in the northwest of India, I met a missionary from New Zealand who had been involved in Christian ministry in India for 25 years. During her final term, she was assigned to a Christian bookstore. One day as my team and I went to her shop to buy some books, we found the bookshop closed. When we went to her missionary quarters—which were in a walled mansion—we asked what was happening. She replied, "I am going back home for good."

I asked what would happen to the ministry of the bookshop. She answered, "I have sold all the books at wholesale price, and I have closed down everything."

With deep hurt, I asked her if she could have handed the store over to someone in order to continue the work.

"No, I could not find anyone," she replied. I wondered why, after 25 years of being in India, she was leaving without one person whom she had won to Christ, no disciple to continue her work. She, along with her missionary colleagues, lived in walled compounds with three or four servants each to look after their lifestyle. She spent a lifetime and untold amounts of God's precious money, which could have been used to preach the Gospel. I could not help but think Jesus had called us to become servants—not masters. Had she done so, she would have fulfilled the call of God upon her life and fulfilled the Great Commission.

Unfortunately, this sad truth is being repeated all over the world of colonial-style foreign missions. Regrettably, seldom are traditional missionaries being held accountable for the current lack of results, nor is their failure being reported at home in the West.

At the same time, native evangelists are seeing thousands turn to Christ in revival movements on every continent. Hundreds of new churches are being formed every week by native missionaries in the Two-Thirds World!

Nineteen

The Church's Primary Task

God obviously is moving mightily among native believers. These are the wonderful, final days of Christian history. Now is the time for the whole family of God to unite and share with one another as the New Testament Church did, the richer churches giving to the poorer.

The Body of Christ in the East is looking to the West to link hands with them in this time of harvest and to support the work with the material blessings that God has showered upon them. With the love and support of North American believers, we can help native evangelists and their families march forward and complete the task of world evangelization in this century.

As I sit on platforms and stand in pulpits all across North America, I am speaking on behalf of the native brethren. God has called me to be the servant of the needy brothers who cannot speak up for themselves in North America.

As I wait to speak, I look out over the congregation, and I often pray for some of the missionaries by name. Usually I pray something like this: "Lord Jesus, I am about to stand here on behalf of Thomas John and P.T. Steven tonight. May I represent them faithfully. Help us meet their needs through this meeting."

Of course, the names of the native missionaries change each time. But I believe the will of God will not be accomplished in our generation unless this audience and many others like it respond to the cry of the lost. Each of us must follow the Lord in the place to which He has called us—the native evangelist in his land and the sponsors here in this land. Some obey by going; others obey by supporting. Even if you cannot go to Asia, you can fulfill the Great Commission by helping send native brothers to the pioneer fields.

This and many other similar truths about missions are no longer understood in the West. Preaching and teaching about missions has been lost in most of our churches. The sad result is seen everywhere. Most believers no longer can define what a missionary is, what he or she does or what the work of the Church is as it relates to the Great Commission.

A declining interest in missions is the sure sign that a church and people have left their first love. Nothing is more indicative of the moral decline of the West than Christians who have lost the passion of Christ for a lost and dying world.

The older I become, the more I understand the real reason millions go to hell without hearing the Gospel.

Actually, this is not a mission problem. As I said earlier, it is a theological problem—a problem of misunderstanding and unbelief. Many churches have slipped so far from biblical teaching that Christians cannot explain why the Lord left us here on earth.

All of us are called for a purpose. Some years ago when I was in North India, a little boy about eight years old watched me as I prepared for my morning meditations. I began to talk to him about Jesus and asked him several questions.

"What are you doing?" I asked the lad.

"I go to school," was the reply.

"Why do you go to school?"

"To study," he said.

"Why do you study?"

"To get smart."

"Why do you want to get smart?"

"So I can get a good job."

"Why do you want to get a good job?"

"So I can make lots of money."

"Why do you want to make lots of money?"

"So I can buy food."

"Why do you want to buy food?"

"So I can eat."

"Why do you want to eat?"

"To live."

"Why do you live?"

At that point, the little boy thought for a minute, scratched his head, looked me in the face and said, "Sir, why do I live?" He paused a moment in mid thought, then gave his own sad answer, "To die!"

The question is the same for all of us: Why do we live?

What is the basic purpose of your living in this world, as you claim to be a disciple of the Lord Jesus Christ? Is it to accumulate wealth? Fame? Popularity? To fulfill the desires of the flesh and of the mind? And to somehow survive and, in the end, to die and hopefully go to heaven?

No. The purpose of your life as a believer must be to obey Jesus when He said, "Go ye into all the world, and preach the gospel. . . . " That is what Paul did when he laid down his arms and said, "Lord, what do You want me to do?"

If all of your concern is about your own life, your job, your clothes, your children's good clothes, healthy bodies, a good education, a good job and marriage, then your concerns are no different from a heathen's in Bhutan, Myanmar or India.

In recent months I have looked back on those seven years of village evangelism as one of the greatest learning experiences of my life. We walked in Jesus' steps, incarnating and representing Him to masses of people who had never heard the Gospel.

When Jesus was here on earth, His goal was to do nothing but the will of His Father. Our commitment must be only His will. Jesus no longer is walking on earth. We are His body; He is our head. That means our lips are the lips of Jesus. Our hands are His hands; our eyes, His eyes; our hope, His hope. My wife and children belong to Jesus. My money, my talent, my education—all belong to Jesus.

So what is His will? What are we to do in this world with all of these gifts He has given us?

"As my Father hath sent me, even so send I you," are His instructions. "Go ye therefore, and teach all nations, baptizing them in the name of the Father, and of the Son, and of the Holy Ghost: Teaching them to observe all things whatsoever I have commanded you: and, lo, I am with you alway, even unto the end of the world" (John 20:21; Matthew 28:19–20).

Every Christian should know the answers to the following three basic questions about missions in order to fulfill the call of our Lord to reach the lost world for His name.

One, what is the primary task of the Church? Each of the four Gospels—Matthew, Mark, Luke and John—gives us a mandate from our Lord Jesus, the mission statement of the Church, known as the Great Commission. See Matthew 28:18–20; Mark 16:15–16; Luke 24:47; and John 20:21.

The Great Commission reveals the reason God has left us here in this world, the main activity of the Church until Jesus returns as the King of kings to gather us to Himself. He desires us to go everywhere proclaiming the love of God to a lost world. Exercising His authority and demonstrating His power, we are to preach the Gospel, make disciples, baptize and teach people to obey all the commands of Christ.

This task involves more than handing out leaflets, holding street meetings or showing compassionate love to the sick and hungry, although these may be involved. But the Lord wants us to continue as His agents to redeem and transform the lives of people. Disciple making, as Jesus defined it, obviously involves the long-time process of planting local churches.

Note too that the references to the Great Commission are accompanied by promises of divine power. The global expansion of the Church obviously is a task for a special people who are living intimately enough with God to discern and exercise His authority.

Two, who is a missionary? A missionary is anyone sent by the Lord to establish a new Christian witness where such a witness is yet unknown. Traditionally defined missionary activity usually involves leaving our own immediate culture for another, taking the Gospel to people who differ in at least one aspect—such as language, nationality, race or tribe—from our own ethnic group.

For some reason, many North Americans have come to believe that a missionary is only someone from the West who goes to Asia, Africa or some other foreign land. Not so. When a former Hindu Brahmin crosses the subtle caste lines of India and works among low-caste people, he should be recognized as a missionary just as much as a person who goes from Detroit to Calcutta.

Christians in the West must abandon the totally unscriptural idea that they should support only white missionaries from America. Today it is essential that we support missionaries going from South India to North India, from one island of the Philippines to another or from Korea to China.

Unless we abandon the racism implied in our unwritten definition of a missionary, we never will see the world reached for Christ. While governments may close the borders of their countries to Western missionaries, they cannot close them to their own people. The Lord is raising up such an army of national missionaries right now, but they cannot go unless

North Americans will continue to support the work as they did when white Westerners were allowed.

Three, where is the mission field? One of the biggest mistakes we make is to define mission fields in terms of nation states. These are only political boundaries established along arbitrary lines through wars or by natural boundaries such as mountain ranges and rivers.

A more biblical definition conforms to linguistic and tribal groupings. Thus, a mission field is defined as any cultural group that does not have an established group of disciples. The Arabs of New York City, for example, or the people of the Hopi Indian tribe in Dallas are unreached people groups in the United States. More than 10,000 such hidden people groups worldwide represent the real pioneer mission fields of our time.[1]

They will be reached only if someone from outside their culture is willing to sacrifice his or her own comfortable community to reach them with the Gospel of Christ. And to go and do so, that person needs believers at home who will stand behind him with prayers and finances. The native missionary movement in Asia—because it is close at hand to most of the world's unreached peoples—can most easily send the evangelists. But they cannot always raise the needed support among their destitute populations. This is where Christians in the West can come forward, sharing their abundance with God's servants in Asia.

Missionary statesman George Verwer believes most North American Christians are still only playing soldiers. But he also believes, as I do, that across America individuals and groups want to arouse the sleeping giant in our nation to support the missionaries needed for Asian evangelization. We should not rest until the task is complete.

You may never be called personally to reach the hidden peoples of Asia; but through soldier-like suffering at home, you can make it possible for millions to hear overseas.

Today I am calling on Christians to give up their stale Christianity, use the weapons of spiritual warfare and advance against the enemy. We must stop skipping over the verses that read, "If any man will come after me, let him deny himself, and take up his cross, and follow me," and "So likewise, whosoever he be of you that forsaketh not all that he hath, he cannot be my disciple" (Matthew 16:24; Luke 14:33).

Were these verses written only for the native missionaries who are on the front lines being stoned and beaten and going hungry for their faith? Or were they written only for North American believers comfortably going through the motions of church, teaching conferences and concerts?

Of course not. These verses apply equally to Christians in Bangkok, Boston and Bombay. Says Verwer,

> Some missionary magazines and books leave one with the impression that worldwide evangelization is only a matter of time. More careful research will show that in densely populated areas the work of evangelism is going backward rather than forward.
>
> In view of this, our tactics are simply crazy. Perhaps 80 percent of our efforts for Christ—weak as they often are—still are aimed at only 20 percent of the world's population. Literally hundreds of millions of dollars are poured into every kind of Christian project at home, especially buildings, while only a thin trickle goes out to the regions beyond. Half-hearted saints believe by giving just a few hundred dollars they have done their share. We all have measured ourselves so long by the man next to us we barely can see the standard set by men like Paul or by Jesus Himself.
>
> During the Second World War, the British showed themselves capable of astonishing sacrifices (as did many other nations). They lived on meager, poor rations. They cut down their railings and sent them for weapons manufacture. Yet today, in what is more truly a (spiritual) World War, Christians live as peacetime soldiers. Look at Paul's injunctions to Timothy in 2 Timothy 2:3–4: "Thou therefore endure hardness, as a good soldier of

Jesus Christ. No man that warreth entangleth himself with the affairs of this life; that he may please him who hath chosen him to be a soldier." We seem to have a strange idea of Christian service. We will buy books, travel miles to hear a speaker on blessings, pay large sums to listen to a group singing the latest Christian songs—but we forget that we are soldiers.[2]

Day after day I continue with this one message: Hungry, hurting native missionaries are waiting to go to the next village with the Gospel, but they need your prayer and financial support. We are facing a new day in missions, but it requires the cooperation of Christians in both the East and West.

Twenty

"Lord, Help Us Remain True to You"

Yes, today God is working in a miraculous way. Without all the trappings of high powered promotion, an increasing number of believers are catching the vision of God's third wave in missions. We already have seen thousands of individuals raised up to share in the work. But I believe this is also only a foretaste of the millions more who will respond in the days ahead. Many pastors, church leaders, former missionaries and Christian broadcasters in North America are also unselfishly lending their support.

In addition to these sponsors and donors, volunteers are coordinating efforts at the grassroots level throughout the United States and Canada. This network of local workers is making a tremendous contribution in fulfilling the Great Commission. They represent Gospel for Asia at conferences and distribute literature to friends. They show GFA videos and share what the Lord is doing through native missionaries with churches, Sunday schools, home Bible studies, prayer meetings and other Christian gatherings. By recruiting additional senders, they multiply what they could have given on their own.

I will never forget one dear retired widow whom I met on a speaking tour. Excited about how much she still could do even though she wasn't working, she pledged to sponsor a missionary out of her tiny Social Security check.

After six months I received a very sad letter from her. "Brother K.P.," she wrote, "I am so privileged to be supporting a missionary. I'm living all alone now on only a fixed income. I know when I get to heaven I'm going to meet people who have come to Christ through my sharing, but I must reduce my support because my utility bills have gone up. Please pray for me that I will find a way to give my full support again."

When my wife, Gisela, showed me the letter, I was deeply touched. I called the woman and told her she need not feel guilty—she was doing all she could. I even advised her not to give if it became a greater hardship.

Two weeks later, another letter came. "Every day," she wrote, "I've been praying for a way to find some more money for my missionary. As I prayed, the Lord showed me a way—I've disconnected my phone."

I looked at the check. Tears came to my eyes as I thought how much this woman was sacrificing. She must be lonely, I thought. What would happen if she got sick? Without a phone, she would be cut off from the world. "Lord," I prayed, as I held the check in both hands, "help us to remain true to You and honor this great sacrifice."

Another gift, this time from a 13-year-old boy named Tommy, shows the same spirit of sacrifice. For more than a year, Tommy had been saving for a new bicycle for school. Then he read about the value of bicycles to native missionaries like Mohan Ram and his wife from Tamil Nadu state. Since 1977, Mohan had been walking in the scorching sun between villages, engaged with his wife in church planting, through Bible classes, open-air evangelism, tract distribution, children's ministry and Bible translation. He and his family lived in one rented room and had to walk for miles or ride buses to do Gospel work. A bicycle would mean more to him than a car would mean to someone in suburban America.

But a new Indian-made bicycle, which would cost only $92, was totally out of reach of his family's budget. What amazed me when I came to the United States is that bikes here are considered children's toys or a way to lose weight. For native missionaries they represent a way to expand the ministry greatly and reduce suffering.

When Tommy heard that native missionaries use their bikes to ride 17 to 20 miles a day, he made a big decision. He decided to give to GFA the bike money he had saved.

"I can use my brother's old bike," he wrote. "My dad has given me permission to send you my new bike money for the native missionary."

Some people find unusual ways to raise extra native missionary support. One factory worker goes through all the trashcans at his workplace collecting aluminum beverage cans. Each month we get a check from him—usually enough to sponsor two or more missionaries.

One pastor, whose Southwest congregation numbers more than 12,000, personally supports several native missionaries. Like other pastors, he has been overseas to learn about the work of native missionaries. In addition to his congregation's monthly support, he has had GFA staff make several presentations at the church. As a result, several hundred families also have taken on sponsorship. Through his influence, a number of other pastors also have started to include GFA in their regular mission budgets.

A young woman whose missionary parents have served in India for 30 years said, "I always wondered why my parents didn't see people coming to Jesus in their work. Now I'm glad I can sponsor a native missionary who is fruitful."

Support for the work of Gospel for Asia has come from other Christian organizations in the United States in some unique ways. For example, we were invited to participate in the Keith

Green Memorial Concert Tour as the official representative of Two-Thirds World missions.

One of GFA's dearest friends has been David Mains of Mainstay Ministries in Wheaton, Illinois. Through my guest visits on his radio broadcasts, sponsors have joined our family from all over the United States. David and his wife, Karen, have advised and helped us in a number of much-needed areas—including the publishing of this book.

Although David and Karen never have said anything about sacrificial giving, I know they have helped us during periods when their own ministry was experiencing financial stress. But Scripture is true when it says, "Give, and it shall be given unto you . . . " (Luke 6:38). One of the unchanging laws of the kingdom is that we must always be giving away from ourselves—both in good times and bad. How many North American churches, Christian ministries and individuals are experiencing financial difficulties because they have disobeyed these clear commands of God to share?

I could list many others who have helped, but one more whom I must mention is Bob Walker, long-time publisher and editor. Sensitive to the Holy Spirit, Bob prayed about us and said he felt led of God to run articles and reports on the work. He also shared his mailing list with us, endorsing our ministry and urging his readers to support the native missionary movement when many others took a wait-and-see attitude toward our new ministry.

This kind of openhanded sharing helped launch Gospel for Asia in the beginning and keeps us growing now. In our weekly nights of prayer and in regular prayer meetings, we constantly remember to thank God for these kinds of favors—and pray that more leaders will be touched with the need to share their resources with the Two-Thirds World.

Perhaps the most exciting long-range development has been

ABOVE: THESE GOSPEL FOR ASIA MISSIONARIES are involved in reaching the unreached in Nepal's mountain regions. They often must hike dangerous mountain trails, risking their very lives to reach the unreached.

RIGHT: EVERY YEAR, Gospel for Asia produces over 300 million pieces of literature in 18 different languages to reach the multitudes who are desperately hungry for the Gospel.

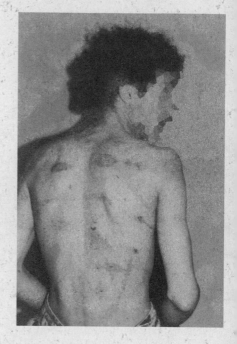

RIGHT: **EVERY YEAR,** dozens of native missionaries are beaten for preaching the Gospel. Some must be hospitalized, and a few are even martyred for the sake of Christ. But they still go out, knowing the risks, their hearts burdened to bring the message of Jesus Christ to the lost areas of Asia.

BELOW: **GFA'S VAN TEAMS** are one of the ministry's most powerful evangelism tools. Equipped with Christian literature, the life of Jesus film, a generator, and a megaphone, they travel from village to village, preaching the Gospel and planting churches.

ABOVE: NATIVE MISSIONARIES MUST OFTEN WALK 10 to 15 miles to reach a single unreached village. Bicycles enable them to reach dozens. Every year Gospel for Asia buys several thousand bicycles, enabling missionaries to go farther, sooner.

LEFT: WITH A 60 TO 80 PERCENT ILLITERACY RATE in many parts of the Subcontinent, flip charts like this one clearly communicate the Gospel. These villagers listen eagerly as the native missionary explains about the Lord Jesus Christ. Often, right there on the street, they will receive Jesus in their hearts.

RIGHT: **RADIO** is an extremely effective means to reach the unreached. In cooperation with international broadcasters, Gospel for Asia produces daily broadcasts in 83 different languages. In response, more than 50,000 people write every month, asking for more information about the Lord.

BELOW: **A FAMILY LISTENS** to Gospel for Asia's Nepali broadcast. Every year, in remote areas throughout the mission field, churches are planted through GFA's radio broadcasts. Millions of people hear the name of Jesus through this medium.

a slow but steady shift in the attitude of North American mission agencies and denominations toward native mission movements.

One after another, older missions and denominations have changed anti-native policies and are beginning to support native missionary movements as equal partners in the work of the Gospel. The old racism and colonial mind-set are slowly but surely disappearing.

This, I believe, could have long-range impact. If North American denominations and older mission societies would use their massive networks of support to raise funding for native missions, it would be possible for us and similar native missionary ministries to support several hundred thousand more native missionaries in the Two-Thirds World.

Asks John Haggai, "In a day when an estimated three-fourths of the Third World's people live in countries that either discourage or flatly prohibit foreign missionary efforts, what other way is there to obey Jesus Christ's directive to evangelize all the world? For many thoughtful Christians the answer is becoming more and more clear: In those closed countries, evangelization through trained national Christian leaders is the logical way.... Some observers have gone so far as to say it may be the only way."

The day of the native missionary movement has come. The seeds have been planted. Ahead of us lies much cultivation and nurture, but it can happen if we will share our resources as the apostle Paul outlined in 2 Corinthians 8 and 9. There he urges the wealthy Christians to collect monies and send support to the poor churches in order that equality may abound in the whole Body of Christ. Those who have are obligated to share with those who have not, he argues, because of Christ's example.

"For ye know the grace of our Lord Jesus Christ, that, though he was rich, yet for your sakes he became poor, that ye through his poverty might be rich" (2 Corinthians 8:9). This is the New Testament cry I am repeating to the wealthy and affluent Christians of the West. Many are becoming more willing to follow the example of our Lord Jesus, who made Himself poor for the salvation of others.

How many are ready to live for eternity and follow His example into a more sacrificial lifestyle? How many will join in the spirit of suffering of the native brethren? They are hungry, naked and homeless for the sake of Christ. I do not ask North Americans to join them—sleeping along roadsides and going to prison for their witness. But I do ask believers to share in the most practical ways possible—through financial sharing and intercessory prayer.

One couple caught the message and demonstrated real spiritual understanding. Recently they wrote, "While we were reading your *SEND!* publication, the Lord began to speak to us about going to India. As we pondered this and asked the Lord about it, He spoke again and said, 'You're not going physically, but you're going spiritually and financially.'

"Well, praise the Lord—here is our 'first trip' to India. Please use this money where you see the greatest need. May God's richest blessing be upon you and your ministry."

Enclosed was a check for $1,000. It was signed, "Fellow workers in Christ, Jim and Betty."

My prayer? For several hundred thousand more like Jim and Betty with the spiritual sensitivity to hear what the Lord is really saying today to the North American Church.

Twenty-One

Facing Tests

He smiled warmly at me from across his big polished desk. I was very impressed. This man led one of the greatest ministries in America, one I had admired for years. A great preacher, author and leader, he had a huge following, both among clergy and laypeople.

He had sent me a plane ticket and had invited me to fly across the country to advise him on expanding his work in India. I was flattered. His interest in GFA and the native missionary movement pleased me much more than I was willing to let him believe. From the minute he had first called me, I sensed that this man could be a valuable friend to us in many ways. Perhaps he would open the doors and help us provide sponsorships for some of the hundreds of native missionaries waiting for our support.

But I was not ready for the generous offer he made—one that would turn out to be the first of many tests for me and our mission.

"Brother K.P.," he said slowly, "would you consider giving up what you're doing here in the United States and going back to India as our special representative? We believe that God is calling you to work with us—to take the message of our church back to the people of India. We'll back you up 100 percent to do it.

"You'll have whatever you need," he went on without pausing for breath. "We'll give you a printing press and vans and litera- ture. We're prepared to provide you with all the funding, many times what you can raise yourself."

It was an exciting offer. Then he made it sound even sweeter. "You can give up all this traveling and raising money. You won't need an office and staff in the States. We'll do all that for you. You want to be in Asia, don't you? That's where the work is—so we'll free you to go back and run the work there."

Weakened by the thought of having so many of my prayers answered in one stroke, I let my mind play with the possibili- ties. This could be the biggest answer to prayer we have ever had, I thought. As we talked, my eyes unconsciously wandered across the desk to an album of his best-selling teaching tapes. They were well done, a series on some controversial issues that were sweeping across the United States at that time. They were, however, irrelevant to our needs and problems in Asia.

Seeing what appeared to be my interest in the cassettes, he spoke with a sudden burst of self-assurance. "We'll start with these tapes," he said, handing them to me. "I'll give you the support you need to produce them in India. We can even have them translated in all the major languages. We'll produce mil- lions of copies and get this message into the hands of every Indian believer."

I had heard other men with the same wild idea. The tapes would be useless in India. Millions were going to hell there; they did not need this man's message at all. Although I thought his idea was insane, I tried to be polite.

"Well," I offered lamely, "there might be some material here that could be adapted for India and printed as a booklet."

Suddenly his face froze. I sensed that I had said something wrong.

"Oh, no," he said with an air of stubborn finality, "I can't change a word. That's the message God gave me. It's part of what we're all about. If it's not a problem in India now, it soon will be. We need you to help us get the word out all over Asia."

In an instant this basically good man of God had shown his real colors. His heart was not burning with a passion for the lost at all—or for the churches of Asia. He had an axe to grind, and he thought he had the money to hire me to grind it for him overseas. It was the same old story—a case of religious neocolonialism.

Here I was, face-to-face again with pride and flesh in all its ugliness. I admired and liked this man and his ministry, but he had only one problem. He believed, as many before him have, that if God was doing anything in the world, He would do it through him.

As soon as I could, I excused myself politely and never called him back. He was living in a world of the past, in the day of colonial missions when Western denominations could export and peddle their doctrines and programs to the emerging churches of Asia.

The Body of Christ in Asia owes a great debt to the wonderful missionaries who came in the 19th and 20th centuries. They brought the Gospel to us and planted the Church. But the Church now needs to be released from Western domination.

My message to the West is simple: God is calling Christians everywhere to recognize that He is building His Church in Asia. Your support is needed for the native missionaries whom God is raising up to extend His Church—but not to impose your man-made controls and teachings on the Eastern churches.

Gospel for Asia has faced other tests. Perhaps the biggest came from another group that also shall remain unidentified. This time it involved the biggest single gift ever offered us.

Our friendship and love for members of this group had developed over the previous few years. We have seen God birth into their hearts a burden to see the Gospel of the Lord Jesus preached in the demonstration of the power of God throughout the world. God had given them a desire to be involved in the equipping of native pastors and evangelists, and they had helped GFA financially with projects over the past several years.

Once, by apparent chance, I ran into a delegation of four of their American brothers in India. They had met some of our native missionaries, and I could see they were significantly challenged and deeply touched by the lives of the Indian evangelists. When I returned home, letters of thanks were waiting for me, and a couple of the men offered to sponsor a native missionary. This gesture amazed me because these same men also were voting to give us financial grants for other projects. It convinced me they really believed in the work of the native brethren—enough to get personally involved beyond their official duties as trustees.

Imagine the way I shouted and danced around the office when I got another call from the chairman of this board two weeks later. They had decided, he said, to give us a huge amount from their missionary budget! I could barely imagine a gift of that size. When I hung up the phone, the staff in our office thought I had gone crazy. How desperately we needed that money. In fact, in my mind I already had it spent. The first part would go, I thought, to start an intensive missionary training institute for new missionaries.

Perhaps that is why the next development was such a blow. As members of their board discussed the project among themselves, questions arose about accountability and control. They phoned me, expressing that the only way the board would agree to support the project would be for a representative of their organization to be on the board of the institute in India. After all, they said, that large amount of money just could not be released with "no strings attached."

The request went through my heart like a knife. This was a real surprise. Through all the years, I always personally had refused to sit on any of the native mission boards we support in Asia. We always have given our aid without demanding control of an indigenous ministry. To suggest that an outsider sit on the board of this new indigenous work would betray my brethren and take them back into bondage of men.

Taking a deep breath and asking the Lord for help, I tried to explain our GFA policy.

"Our leaders overseas fast and pray about every decision," I said. "We don't have to sit on their boards to protect our monies. It's not our money, anyway; it belongs to God. He is greater than GFA or your organization. Let God protect His own interests. The native brethren don't need you or me to be their leader. Jesus is their Lord, and He will lead them in the right way to use the grant."

The silence on the other end of the line was long.

"I'm sorry, Brother K.P.," said the director finally. "I don't think I can sell this idea to our board of directors. They want accountability for the money. How can they have that without putting a man on the board? Be reasonable. You're making it very hard on us to help. This is standard policy for a gift of this size."

My mind raced. A little voice said, "Go ahead. All they want is a worthless piece of paper. Don't make an issue of this. After all, this is the biggest grant you've ever received. Nobody gives big money away like this without some control. Stop being a fool."

But I knew I could not consent to that proposal. I could not face the Asian brethren and say that in order to get this money, they had to have an American fly halfway around the world to approve how they spent it.

"No," I said, "we cannot accept your money if it means compromising the purity of our ministry. We have plenty of accountability through the trusted godly men who have been appointed to the native board. Later, you can see the building yourself when you go to Asia. I can't compromise the autonomy of the work by putting an American on the native board. What you are suggesting is that you want to 'steady the ark' as Uzzah did in the Old Testament. God slew him because he presumed to control the working of God. When the Holy Spirit moves and does His work, we become restless because we want to control it. It is an inherent weakness of the flesh. The bottom line of your offer is to control the work in Asia with hidden strings attached to your gift. You have to learn to let your money go, because it is not your money but God's."

Then, with my heart in my mouth, I gave him one last argument, hoping it could save the gift—but willing to lose all if I was unable to convince them.

"Brother," I said quietly, "I sign checks for hundreds of thousands of dollars and send them to the field every month. Many times as I hold those big checks in my hand, I pray, 'Lord, this is Your money. I'm just a steward sending it where You said it should go. Help the leaders on the field use this money to win the lost millions and glorify the name of Jesus.' All we must be concerned about is doing our part. I obey the Holy Spirit in dispensing the Lord's money. Don't ask me to ask the native brethren to do something I won't do."

I paused. What more could I say?

"Well," the voice at the other end of the line repeated, "we really want to help. I will make the presentation, but you're making it very hard for me."

"I'm sure," I said with conviction, "there are other organizations that will meet your requirement. I just know we can't. Fellowship in the Gospel is one thing—but outside control is unbiblical and in the end harms the work more than helping it."

I said it with conviction, but inside I was sure we had lost the grant. There was nothing more to say but good-bye.

Two weeks passed without a contact. Every day I prayed God would help the whole board of directors understand. Our inner circle—people who knew about the expected gift—kept asking me if I had heard anything. Our whole office was praying.

"We're walking in the narrow way," I said bravely to the staff, "doing what God has told us." Inside I kept wishing God would let me bend the rules a little this time.

But our faithfulness paid off. One day the phone rang, and it was the director again. The board had met the night before, and he had presented my position to them.

"Brother K P," he said with a smile in his voice, "we have met and discussed the project quite extensively. I shared the importance of autonomy of the national brothers. They have voted unanimously to go ahead and support the project without controls."

There is no guarantee you will always have that kind of happy ending when you stand up for what is right. But it does not matter. God has called us to be here in the West, challenging the affluent people of this world to share with those in the most desperate need of all.

God is calling Christians in the West to recognize that He is building His Church as a caring, sharing and saving outreach to dying souls. He is using many North Americans who care about the lost to share in this new movement by supporting the native missionary leaders He has called to direct it.

God is calling the Body of Christ in the affluent West to give up its proud, arrogant attitude of "our way is the only way" and share with those who will die in sin unless help is sent now from the richer nations. The West must share with the East, knowing that Jesus said, "Inasmuch as ye have done it unto one of the least of these my brethren, ye have done it unto me" (Matthew 25:40).

Have native missionaries made mistakes? Yes. And it would be unwise stewardship to give away our money freely without knowledge of the truthfulness and integrity of any ministry. But that does not mean we should not help the native missionary movement.

North America is at the crossroads. We can harden our hearts to the needs of the Two-Thirds World—continuing in arrogance, pride and selfishness—or we can repent and move with the Spirit of God. Whichever way we turn, the laws of God will continue in effect. If we close our hearts to the lost of the world who are dying and going to hell, we invite the judgment of God and a more certain ruin of our affluence. But if we open our hearts and share, it will be the beginning of new blessing and renewal.

This is why I believe that the response of North American believers is crucial. This cry of my heart is more than a mission question that can be shrugged off like another appeal letter or banquet invitation. Response to the needs of the lost world is directly tied to the spiritual beliefs and well-being of every believer. Meanwhile, the unknown brethren of Asia continue to lift hands to God in prayer, asking Him to meet their needs. They are men and women of the highest caliber. They cannot be bought. Many have developed a devotion to God that makes them hate the idea of becoming servants of men and religious establishments for profit.

They are the true brethren of Christ about which the Bible speaks, walking from village to village facing beatings and per-secution to bring Christ to animists, Buddhists, communists, Hindus, Muslims and many other people who have still not received the Good News of His love.

Without fear of men they are willing, like their Lord, to live as He did—sleeping on roadsides, going hungry and even dying in order to share their faith. They go even though they may be told the mission fund is used up. They are determined to preach even though they know it will mean suffering. Why? Because they love the lost souls who are dying daily without Christ. They are too busy doing the will of God to get involved in church politics, board meetings, fund-raising campaigns and public relations efforts.

It is the highest privilege of affluent Christians in the West to share in their ministries by sending financial aid. If we do not care enough to sponsor them—if we do not obey the love of Christ and send them support—we are sharing in the responsibility for those who go to eternal flames without ever hearing about the love of God. If native evangelists cannot go because no one will send them, the shame belongs to the Body of Christ here because it has the funds to help them. And if those funds are not given to the Lord, they soon will disappear. If the Western Church will not be a light to the world, the Lord will take their candlestick away.

Pretending the poor and lost do not exist may be an alternative. But averting our eyes from the truth will not eliminate our guilt. Gospel for Asia exists to remind the affluent Christian that there is a hungry, needy, lost world of people out there whom Jesus loves and for whom He died. Will you join us in ministering to them?

Twenty-Two

The Vision of Asia's Lost Souls

Many Westerners concerned about missions have grown up hearing the classic approach: "Send Americans." They never have been asked to consider alternatives better suited to changed geopolitical conditions. It is hard for some to hear me reinterpret the stories told by Western missionaries of hardship and fruitless ministry as indicators of outdated and inappropriate methods.

But the biggest hurdle for most North Americans is the idea that someone from somewhere else can do it better. Questions about our methods and safeguards for financial accountability, although often sincere and well-intentioned, sometimes emanate from a deep well of distrust and prejudice.

On one of my trips to the West Coast, I was invited to meet with the mission committee of a church that supported more than 75 American missionaries. After I shared our vision for supporting native missionaries, the committee chairman said, "We have been asked to support national missionaries before, but we haven't found a satisfactory way to hold these nationals accountable for either the money we send or the work they do." I sensed he spoke for the entire committee.

I could hardly wait to respond. This issue of accountability is the objection most often raised about supporting native missionaries to the Two-Thirds World, and I can understand why.

Indeed, I agree it is extremely important that there be adequate accountability in every area of ministry. Good stewardship demands it.

So I detailed how we handle the subject.

"In order to make people accountable, we need some norm by which to measure their performance," I said. "But what criteria should we use? Would the yearly independent audit our missionaries submit be adequate to see that they handled money wisely?"

I raised other questions. "What about the churches they build or the projects they have undertaken? Should they be judged according to the patterns and goals some mission headquarters or denominations prescribed? What about the souls they've won and the disciples they've made? Would any denomination have criteria to evaluate those? How about criteria to evaluate their lifestyle on the field or the fruit they produce? Which of these categories should be used to make these native missionaries accountable?"

Those who had been leaning back in their chairs now were leaning forward. I had laid a foundation for a thought I was sure they hadn't considered before. I continued: "Do you require the American missionaries you send overseas to be accountable to you? What criteria have you used in the past to account for the hundreds of thousands of dollars you have invested through the missionaries you support now?"

I looked to the chairman for an answer. He stumbled through a few phrases before admitting they never had thought of requiring American missionaries to be accountable, nor was this ever a concern to them.

"The problem," I explained, "is not a matter of accountability but one of prejudice, mistrust and feelings of superiority. These are the issues that hinder love and support for our brothers in the Two-Thirds World who are working to win their own people to Christ." I followed with this illustration:

"Three months ago, I traveled to Asia to visit some of the brothers we support. In one country I met an American missionary who had for 14 years been developing some social programs for his denomination. He had come to this country hoping he could establish his mission center, and he had been successful. As I walked into his mission compound, I passed a man with a gun, sitting at the gate. The compound was bordered by a number of buildings with at least half-a-dozen imported cars. The staff members were wearing Western clothes, and a servant was caring for one of the missionary children. The scene reminded me of a king living in a palace with his court of serfs caring for his every need. I have, in 18 years of travel, seen this scene repeated many times.

"From conversation with some of the native missionaries," I continued, "I learned that this American and his colleagues did live like kings with their servants and cars. They had no contact with the poor in the surrounding villages. God's money is invested in missionaries like this who enjoy a lifestyle they could not afford in the United States—a lifestyle of a rich man, separated by economy and distance from the native missionaries walking barefoot, poorly dressed even by their own standards and sometimes going for days without eating. These nationals, in my opinion, are the real soldiers of the cross. Each one of the brothers we support in that country has established a church in less than 12 months, and some have started more than 20 churches in three years."

I told of another incident from my own country of India. Although India is closed to new missionaries, some Western missionaries still live there from past times, and some denominations get a few new professional people in, such as doctors or teachers. I visited one of the mission hospitals in India where some of these missionary doctors and their colleagues worked.

All lived in richly furnished mansions. One had 12 servants to care for him and his family: one to look after the garden, another to care for the car, another to care for the children, two to cook in his kitchen, one to take care of his family's clothes, and so on. And in eight years, this missionary had won no one to Jesus nor established one church.

"What criteria," I dared to ask, "has been used by the two evangelical denominations that have sent these men to hold them accountable?

"In another place," I continued, "there is a hospital that cost millions to build and more millions to keep staffed with Europeans and Americans. In 75 years, not one living, New Testament-type church has been established there. Did anyone ever ask for an account of such fruitless labor?

"These illustrations are not isolated instances," I assured my audience. "During my 18 years of travel throughout Asia, I have seen Western missionaries consistently living at an economic level many times above the people among whom they work. And the nationals working with them are treated like servants and live in poverty while these missionaries enjoy the luxuries of life."

I contrasted these examples with what the nationals are doing.

"Remember the illustration of the multi-million dollar hospital and no church?" I asked. "Well, four years ago we began supporting a native missionary and 30 coworkers who have started a mission only a few miles from the hospital. His staff has grown to 349 coworkers, and hundreds of churches have been started. Another native missionary, one of his coworkers, has established more than 30 churches in three years. Where do these brothers live? In little huts just like the people with whom they work. I could give you hundreds of stories that illustrate the fruit of such dedicated lives. It is like the book of Acts being written once again.

"You are seeking accountability from native missionaries, accountability that is required for you to give them support? Remember that Jesus said, 'For John came neither eating nor drinking, and they say, He hath a devil. The Son of man came eating and drinking, and they say, Behold a man gluttonous, and a winebibber, a friend of publicans and sinners. But wisdom is justified of her children' (Matthew 11:18–19).

"Fruit," I pointed out, "is the real test. 'By their fruits ye shall know them,' Jesus said (Matthew 7:20). Paul told Timothy to do two things regarding his life. And these two things, I believe, are the biblical criteria for accountability. He told Timothy to watch his own life and to care for the ministry that was committed to him. The life of the missionary is the medium of his message."

Three hours had passed, yet the room remained quiet. I sensed I had their permission to continue.

"You asked me to give you a method to hold our native missionaries accountable. Apart from the issues I have raised, Gospel for Asia does have definite procedures to ensure that we are good stewards of the monies and opportunities the Lord commits to us. But our requirements and methods reflect a different perspective and way of doing missions.

"First, Gospel for Asia assumes that we who are called, are called to serve and not to be served. We walk before the millions of poor and destitute in Asia with our lives as an open testimony and example. We breathe, sleep and eat conscious of the perishing millions the Lord commands us to love and rescue."

Then I explained how God is reaching the lost, not through programs but through individuals whose lives are so committed to Him that He uses them as vessels to anoint a lost world. So we give top priority to how the missionaries and their leaders live. When we started to support one brother, he lived in two small rooms with concrete floors. He, his wife and four children slept on a mat on the floor.

That was four years ago. On a recent visit to India, I saw him living in the same place, sleeping on the same mat even though his staff had grown from 30 to 349 workers. He handles hundreds of thousands of dollars to keep this enormous ministry going, yet his lifestyle has not changed. The brothers he has drawn into the ministry are willing to die for Christ's sake because they have seen their leader sell out to Christ just as the apostle Paul did.

"In the West, people look to men with power and riches. In Asia, our people look for men like Gandhi who, to inspire a following, was willing to give up all to become like the least of the poor. Accountability begins with the life of the missionary.

"The second criteria we consider," I explained, "is the fruitfulness of that life. Our investment of money shows in the result of lives changed and churches established. What greater accountability can we require?

"When Western missionaries go into Two-Thirds World countries, they are able to find nationals to follow them. But these nationals too often get caught up in denominational distinctives. Like produces like. Missionary leaders from denominations who fly into these countries and live in five-star hotels will draw to themselves so-called national leaders who are like themselves. Then, unfortunately, it is the so-called national leaders who are accused of wasting or misusing great amounts of money, while they have often merely followed the example provided by their Western counterparts."

Again I addressed the chairman: "Have you studied the lives and ministries of the American missionaries you support? I believe you will find that very few of them are directly involved in preaching Christ but are doing some sort of social work. If you apply the biblical principles I have outlined, I doubt you would support more than a handful of them."

Then I turned and asked the committee members to assess

themselves. "If your life is not totally committed to Christ, you are not qualified to be on this committee. That means you cannot use your time, your talents or your money the way you want to. If you do and still think you can help direct God's people to reach a lost world, you mock God Himself. You have to evaluate how you spend every dollar and everything else you do in the light of eternity. The way each one of you lives is where we begin our crusade to reach the lost of this world."

I was gratified to see that the Lord spoke to many of them. There were tears and a feeling of Christ's awareness among us. This had been a painful time for me, and I was glad when it was over. But I needed to be faithful to God's call on my life to share the vision of Asia's lost souls with the affluent Western Christian brothers and sisters who have it in their power to help.

Conclusion

Bihar, the North Indian state known as the graveyard of missions—how can I ever forget the summer months I spent there with Operation Mobilization outreach teams! We were driven out from many villages and stoned for preaching the Gospel. That was in 1968.

Made up of primitive villages with 75 million inhabitants, Bihar is said to be one of the most unreached regions in the world. In 1993, Gospel for Asia began a missionary Bible college in Ranchi, Bihar, to train and send out missionaries to this spiritually needy area.

Brother Simon Kujur was one of the young people who attended. In all of our schools, we strongly encourage our students to pray and seek God's face as to where He wants them to go when they finish their training. While he was studying at the Bible college, Simon prayed that the Lord would guide him to a place where he could reach the lost and plant at least one local church. The Lord placed a special burden on his heart for a specific people group in Bihar; and after his graduation, Simon was sent there, to serve and reach these souls for whom he had prayed.

Three years later, he had already established five churches! All this began with the conversion of one lady named Manjula.

Over the years, Manjula had earned the reputation of a holy woman in her village. Many villagers became her followers and came to her for counsel. They would bring gifts and sacrifices to her because she was a priestess of the goddesses Kali and Durga. She had the reputation for doing many miracles, even causing sickness and death through her powers.

When Simon arrived in that area, people told him about Manjula and the powerful woman she was, with all her magical powers and these powerful goddesses on her side. But then Simon heard that three years before, Manjula had become ill and now was totally paralyzed from the neck down. This young brother realized that this situation was God's appointed opportunity for him to preach the Gospel to her.

Despite the danger to his own life, Simon set out to visit Manjula and talk to her about the Lord Jesus Christ. It was only on his way that he learned more about her story. For weeks, many *pujas*, or ritual prayers with sacrifices, had been carried out for her healing. Hundreds of her followers obeyed her careful instructions to petition her favorite goddesses on her behalf, but nothing had healed her. Recognizing that she must be under attack from evil spirits more powerful than she could handle, she decided to approach even stronger witch doctors to conduct elaborate rituals for her healing. But again, there was no deliverance or hope.

It was at this time that Simon came to her area. When he arrived at her home, he began to witness to her about the Lord Jesus Christ. She listened carefully and told him, "For three years I have tried everything to appease these angry gods. But they don't answer. And now I am confused and terribly frightened."

Simon asked Manjula, "If Jesus would heal you and make you well, what would you do?" Without hesitating she replied, "If your Jesus Christ can heal me and make me well, I will serve

Him the rest of my life." Simon further explained to her about the reality of God's love and how Jesus Christ, the only Savior, could set her free from sin and save her from eternal damnation.

God in His grace opened Manjula's eyes to see the truth. She decided to call upon Jesus to forgive her sin and save her. Simon knelt beside her and prayed for Jesus to heal her. As he prayed aloud, he also fervently prayed in his heart, "Lord Jesus, this may be my only opportunity to see this entire village come to You. Please, Lord, for Your kingdom's sake, touch her and heal her. Your Word says that You will work with me, confirming Your Word, and that miracles would be a sign for these people to believe in You."

As Brother Simon finished praying for Manjula, the power of the Holy Spirit and the grace of God instantly touched her, and she was delivered and healed immediately. Within a few hours she was running around, shouting with joy, "Thank you, Jesus! Thank you, Jesus! Thank you, Jesus!"

Hearing the commotion, a large crowd gathered in front of Manjula's house to see what was going on. There she was, a woman who had been paralyzed for three years, now completely healed. With tears running down her face, she was praising Jesus and shouting His name. Manjula became the first individual in her village to believe in Jesus.

The following week, more than 20 people gave their lives to Christ and were baptized. Manjula opened her house for these new believers to come regularly and worship the Lord Jesus Christ. Just like in Acts 19, when the Ephesian church had its beginning, all evil practices and rituals were completely eradicated; and there was a whole new beginning for this village.

Simon began to preach the Gospel in the neighboring villages as well, and even more people began to come to the Lord Jesus Christ.

Hearing about these events, our leaders from the training center asked Simon if he would visit missionaries in the nearby regions and help them establish churches. Simon began to travel, and now, as a result of his ministry, four more churches have been planted and several new mission stations have opened up. Simon believes this is only the beginning and that even more will happen, with thousands in this area turning to the Lord.

Not long ago, I talked with Simon's leader and asked him, "What is the secret to Simon Kujur's ministry? What is it that causes the Lord to use him so effectively?" Simon's leader replied, "Brother K.P., his case is not an exception. Many of our brothers on the mission field are experiencing the same thing. This is harvest time."

Then he told me something about Simon's life. When he was studying in our Bible college, every morning he would get up early and spend at least three hours with the Lord, on his knees in prayer and meditating on God's Word. When Simon graduated and went to the mission field, he didn't cut back. Instead, the amount of time he spent in prayer increased. Simon doesn't talk publicly about any of these things, but very quietly and humbly goes about preaching the Gospel. Through his life, hundreds are turning to Christ.

Today, just in India alone, nearly 500,000 villages remain without a Christian witness. Add to that countries like Bhutan, Myanmar, Nepal—the entire Subcontinent—where millions and millions live in darkness, waiting for someone like Simon to come and bring the light of the Gospel.

Romans 10:13–17 says that if these multiplied millions sitting in darkness call upon the Lord Jesus Christ, they will be saved. But how can they call on Jesus if they don't believe in Him? And second, how can they believe in Jesus if no one has ever gone to tell them about Him? Finally, you and I are asked this question: How can a person like Simon go unless someone has *sent* him? This is the question we must answer.

Today, God is calling us to become *senders* of missionaries who are waiting to go to these unreached villages. We have a God-given privilege to link our lives with brothers like Simon to see our generation come to know the Lord Jesus Christ.

I encourage you to seek the Lord and see if He is asking you to help support one or more of these native missionaries. If He puts this on your heart, let us know of your decision. You will receive the photograph and testimony of the missionary you are praying for and supporting.

It often takes around $90 to $150 a month to fully support a native missionary, but with as little as $30 a month, you can begin to help support one of these missionaries, sending him to an unreached village that is waiting to hear the Good News. Through your prayers and support, you can help him effectively communicate the Gospel and establish local churches.

Suppose *you* are the one who is privileged to pray and support Simon Kujur as he serves in Bihar. Someday, in eternity, you will stand before the throne with Simon, his family and the thousands who have come to know the Lord through his life and ministry!

Questions and Answers

One of the most meaningful moments in our meetings is the question-and-answer period. Many ask some very provocative questions, which shows they have been thinking seriously about the implications of the message they just heard. Some questions seek details about our policies and practices on the mission field. Certain questions come up repeatedly, and the following are my responses.

QUESTION: What are the qualifications of missionaries you support?

ANSWER: We are looking for those who have a definite call upon their lives to go to the most unreached areas to do evangelism and church planting. It is not a job. A hireling quits when the going gets tough. Our commitment is to train and send out men and women who seek only God's approval and God's glory, those who will not be bought with money or seek their own, even in the work of the Lord.

They must also be people of integrity in the area of commitment to the Word of God and correct doctrine, willing to obey the Scriptures in all matters without question. They must maintain a testimony above reproach, both in their walks with the Lord and also with their families.

We look for those who are willing to work hard to reach the

lost in and around the mission fields on which they are placed. Each missionary is also a shepherd of the flock that the Lord raises up. He will protect these new believers and lead them into maturity in Christ, through teaching God's Word and equipping them to win the lost in these regions.

QUESTION: To whom are native missionary evangelists accountable?

ANSWER: We take several steps to ensure that our accountability systems work without failure. In each area, the missionaries meet at least once a month for a few days of fasting and prayer and sharing together as they build the kingdom in their part of the field. In all cases, native missionaries are supervised by local indigenous elders under whom they work. In turn, these field leaders spend much time meeting with godly senior leaders. These leaders who oversee the ministry are men of integrity and testimony both in their lives and ministries for many years.

QUESTION: Are financial records audited on the field?

ANSWER: Yes, financial records are inspected by our field administrative offices to ensure that funds are used according to the purposes intended. A detailed accounting in writing is required for projects such as village crusades, training conferences and special programs. Missionary support funds are signed for and received both by the leaders and the missionaries involved, and these receipts are checked. All financial records on the field are also audited annually by independent certified public accountants.

QUESTION: It seems the 10/40 Window has become the focus of most mission organizations. What is Gospel for Asia's perspective on reaching the unreached people groups in the 10/40 Window?

ANSWER: In my native language there is this ancient saying: "No picture of a cow in a book is going to go out and eat any grass." There has been a tremendous amount of talk and tons of information pumped out regarding the 10/40 Window and the more than 2 billion people waiting to hear the Gospel. We need to move on from information to implementation if we want to see these people reached with the Gospel.

Ninety-seven percent of the world's unreached people live in this so-called "Resistant Belt." This specific region has become increasingly known as the 10/40 Window. A closer look at the 10/40 Window shows us that there are more unreached people groups in northern India than in any other part of the earth.

Gospel for Asia is more than 25 years old and now supports more than 14,000 native missionaries. These workers live in some of the needy Asian countries, which for the most part are located in the 10/40 Window.

Although from our beginning we have been working among the unreached people in this part of the world, it has only been in the past 10 years or so that we have honed our strategy to reach the most unreached.

Toward the end of the 20th century, serious plans and strategies were developed worldwide by many denominations and agencies to try and finish the task of world evangelism by the year 2000.

All this was exciting; but even after several years into the past decade, how much progress had been made? In 2000 there were 155 discipleship opportunities—offers or invitations to become Christ's disciples—per global inhabitant. Unfortunately, 84 percent of these invitations were extended to people claiming to be Christians and 15.9 percent to people who have already been evangelized, but are non-Christians. Only 0.16 percent were extended to individuals who have never heard the Good News.[1]

The year 2000 has come and gone. Did anything change? Yes—and no. The strategies and initiatives brought about a huge awareness of and motivation for reaching the unreached. But today the goal remains elusive and yet to be achieved.

I believe with all my heart that unless we immediately reverse these numbers by diverting the majority of our re-sources directly to the 10/40 Window, selflessly partner with each other, and find a willingness among local churches to support and encourage indigenous native missionary movements, another year will come and go and nothing will have changed!

This is the reason why the Lord has impressed upon our hearts that we must believe Him to see 100,000 additional missionaries recruited and trained for evangelism and church planting in these most unreached areas.

And just by looking at what the Lord has done through our 54 Bible colleges during these past few years, we are convinced that by the grace of God we will be able to mobilize at least 100,000 radical soldiers in the heart of the 10/40 Window and reach the most unreached.

QUESTION: How are native missionary evangelists trained?

ANSWER: Gospel for Asia has established 54 Bible colleges in the heart of the 10/40 Window. Currently, more than 8,000 students are enrolled, after which they will go to unreached areas to plant churches.

The training for these students is intensive. Their days begin at 5 A.M. The first hour is spent in prayer and meditation on God's Word. Teaching and practical training take place throughout the remainder of the day. Around 11 P.M. their days end.

Each Friday evening is set apart for fasting and more than two hours of prayer. Every weekend the students go to the nearby unreached villages for evangelism. Usually before the end of the school year, they end up starting dozens of house churches and mission stations through these weekend outreach ministries. Before they finish their three-year training, each student will have carefully read through the entire Bible at least three times.

The students spend the first Friday of every month in all-night prayer, praying especially for unreached people groups and other nations. Through these times of prayer, the reality of the lost world becomes very close to their hearts. Throughout the three years at the Bible college, each student is given the opportunity to pray for dozens of totally unreached people groups. At the same time, each one seeks the Lord's face as to where He will have them go to be a missionary.

In all of our training, our first priority is to help these students become more like Christ in their character and nature. The most important thing we want to see happen is that they know the Lord intimately in their lives. Second, we seek to teach them the Word of God in such a way that they are well-equipped, not only to do the work of evangelism, but also to be effective pastors and teachers in the churches they establish. An inductive Bible study course is required for graduation. Third, during their three years, the students receive a tremendous amount of practical training for all aspects of the ministry, including personal evangelism, developing a congregation, and other areas of pastoral care, to help them be effective in the work of the Lord.

QUESTION: Many mission agencies seem to focus only on evangelism, but do not get seriously involved in church planting, as Jesus commanded in the Great Commission. Is GFA just concentrating on evangelism, or are you a church-planting organization?

ANSWER: Reaching the most unreached in our generation—this powerful vision is the single purpose God gave to Gospel for Asia from our very inception.

How could we possibly fulfill such a calling? Most unreached people groups live in the 10/40 Window, in nations that severely restrict or are closed to foreign missionaries. The Lord clearly directed us to use the most effective approach under these circumstances: helping nationals reach their own people and fulfill the Great Commission as commanded in Matthew 28: 19–20. They do this interculturally, near-culturally, and cross-culturally as well.

No doubt the Lord has had His hand on each stage of GFA's growth—from our small beginning, supporting a few workers on the field, to providing tools such as literature and bicycles, then vans, films, projectors and generators. We then began adding thousands of native missionaries in seven different nations to our support list and set up a network of leaders, coordinators and accountability systems.

The Lord enabled GFA to start one radio broadcast in an Indian language and create a follow-up system. Since then, that has expanded to 83 broadcasts, heard daily by millions of people. As part of the follow-up, GFA began producing and distributing books, tracts and other literature.

To mobilize hundreds of new workers for the pioneer fields of Asia, GFA began a three-month intensive missionary training course. This later expanded to a two- to three-year Bible college and has now exploded into 54 Bible colleges and a three-year seminary.

These schools annually produce thousands of new workers to go to the unreached mission fields. As a direct result, GFA has begun a church-planting ministry called Believers Church. This ministry is specifically set up to care for the new converts won by the workers who were sent out from our colleges.

In the past, all these different developments within Gospel for Asia looked like seemingly unrelated puzzle pieces. But now we see that each phase of GFA's growth and expansion was part of a strategic plan. It was the Lord's preparation to bring this ministry to a point at which He could commission us to train and send out 100,000 workers and plant churches in the most unreached areas of the 10/40 Window.

We never imagined that we could come full circle: from a supporting and funding organization to a training and church-planting movement!

You see, in the beginning, we sought only to identify and support existing indigenous groups who were reaching the unreached in their own culture or a nearby culture. We assisted them as much as we could by providing financial help and min-istry tools.

The new direction for our ministry came during a pivotal GFA leaders' meeting in India in 1988. Twenty-five of our leaders met together for a time of serious evaluation and soul-searching to discern if we were indeed reaching the unreached with our efforts.

Our research revealed a harsh reality. The existing missionary force was not effectively targeting those who had never heard the Gospel. That day, after much prayer, we sensed the Lord call-ing us to start a new phase in ministry. As a result, we made a very conscious and deliberate decision to train native missionar-ies and then send them out to plant local churches.

This is how the 54 Bible colleges came into existence. That is why, in villages where no one had ever gone with the name of Jesus, our graduates and workers have now planted more than 21,000 fellowships in the past few years.

As a mission we have come full circle, and we rejoice over the fruit we have already seen. But the majority of the work is yet to be done! Millions are desperately waiting to hear the Gospel.

We are determined to move forward, believing the Lord will indeed enable us to send out 100,000 workers into the ripe har-vest fields of Asia.

QUESTION: What are the methods used by the native missionaries?

ANSWER: Although films, radio, television and video are becoming more common in Asia, the most effective methods still sound more as if they came from the book of Acts!

The most effective evangelism is done face-to-face in the streets. Most native missionaries walk or ride bicycles between villages much like the Methodist circuit riders did in America's frontier days.

Street preaching and open-air evangelism, often using megaphones, are the most common ways to proclaim the Gospel. Sometimes evangelists arrange witnessing parades and/or tent campaigns and distribute simple Gospel tracts during the weeklong village crusades.

Because the majority of the world's 1 billion illiterates live in Asia, the Gospel often must be proclaimed to them without using literature. This is done through showing the film on the life of Jesus and also using cassettes, flip charts and other visual aids to communicate the Gospel.

Trucks, vans, simple loudspeaker systems, bicycles, leaflets, pamphlets, books, banners and flags are the most important tools for our missionaries. Easy to use and train with, they are now being supplemented with radio broadcasting, cassette players, film projectors and television. These types of communication tools are available in Asia at low cost and can be purchased locally without import duties. In addition, native evangelists are familiar with them, and they do not shock the culture.

QUESTION: With your emphasis on the native missionary movement, do you feel there is still a place for Western missionaries in Asia?

ANSWER: Yes, there still are places for Western missionaries. *One, there are still countries with no existing church from which to draw native missionaries.* Morocco, Afghanistan and the Maldive Islands come to mind. In these places, missionaries from outside—whether from the West, Africa or Asia—are a good way for the Gospel to be spread.

Two, Christians in the West have technical skills that may be needed by their brothers and sisters in Two-Thirds World churches. The work of Wycliffe Bible Translators is a good example. Their help in translation efforts in the more than 6,800 languages still without a Bible is invaluable. So when Two-Thirds World churches invite Westerners to come and help them, and the Lord is in it, the Westerners obviously should respond.

Three, there are short-term discipleship experiences that I think are especially valuable. Organizations like Operation Mobilization and Youth With A Mission have had a catalytic impact on both Asian and Western churches. These are discipleship-building ministries that benefit the Western participants as well as Asia's unevangelized millions. I personally was recruited by Operation Mobilization missionaries in 1966 to go to North India.

Through cross-cultural and interracial contact, such ministries are especially helpful because they allow Westerners to get a better understanding of the situation in Asia. Alumni of these programs are helping others in the West understand the real needs of the Two-Thirds World.

And, of course, there is the simple fact that the Holy Spirit does call individuals from one culture to witness to another. When He calls, we should by all means respond.

QUESTION: Why don't indigenous churches support their own missionaries in the Two-Thirds World?

ANSWER: They do. In fact, I believe most Asian Christians give a far greater portion of their income to missions than do Westerners. Scores of times I have seen them give chicken eggs, rice, mangoes and tapioca roots, because they frequently do not have cash. The fact of the matter is that most growing churches in Asia are made up of people from the poor masses. Often they simply do not have money. These are people from among the one-fourth of the world's population who live on less than $1 per day.

Many times we find that a successful missionary evangelist will be almost crippled by his ministry's rapid growth. When a great move of the Holy Spirit occurs in a village, the successful missionary may find he has several trained and gifted coworkers as "Timothys" who are ready to establish sister congregations. However, the rapid growth almost always outstrips the original congregation's ability to support additional workers. This is when outside help is vitally needed.

As God's Spirit continues to move, many new mission boards are being formed. Some of the largest missionary societies in the world are now located in Asia. For example, Gospel for Asia alone currently supports more than 14,000 native missionaries—and this number is increasing at an astonishing rate. But in light of the need, we literally need hundreds of thousands of additional missionaries, who will, in turn, require more outside support.

Regrettably, there are some indigenous churches that do not support native evangelists for the same reason some Western congregations do not give—lack of vision and sin in the lives of the pastors and congregations. But this is no excuse for Western Christians to sit back and lose the greatest opportunity they have ever had to help win a lost world to Jesus.

QUESTION: Is there a danger that native missionary sponsorships will have a reverse effect by causing native evangelists to depend on the West for support rather than turning to the local churches?

ANSWER: The truth is, of course, that it is not outside money that weakens a growing church, but outside control. Money from the West actually liberates the evangelists right now and makes it possible for them to follow the call of God.

After generations of domination by Western colonialists, most Asians are acutely conscious of the potential problem of foreign control through outside money. It is frequently brought up in discussions by native missionary leaders, and most native missionary boards have developed policies and practices to provide for accountability without foreign control.

In Gospel for Asia, we have taken several steps to make sure funds get to the local missionary evangelist in a responsible way without destroying valuable local autonomy.

First, our selection and training process is designed to favor men and women who begin with a right attitude—missionaries who are dependent on God for their support rather than on man.

Second, there is no direct or indirect supervision of the work by Western supporters. The donor gives the Lord's money to the missionary through Gospel for Asia, and we, in turn, send the money to a group of indigenous leaders who oversee the financial affairs on each field. Therefore, the native evangelist is twice-removed from the source of the funds. This procedure is being followed by several other organizations that are collecting funds in the West for native support, and it seems to work very well.

Finally, as soon as a new work is established, the native missionary is able to begin branching out to evangelize nearby unreached villages as well. The new congregations he establishes will eventually gain enough financial stability to fully support him while still giving sacrificially to support evangelism. Eventually, I am sure the native churches will be able to support most pioneer evangelism, but the job is too big now without Western aid.

The quickest way to help Asian churches become self-supporting, I believe, is to support a growing native missionary movement. As new churches are planted, the blessings of the Gospel will abound, and the new Asian believers will be able to support greater outreach. Sponsorship monies are like investment capital in the work of God. The best thing we can do to help make the Asian Church independent now is to support as many native missionaries as possible.

QUESTION: How can Gospel for Asia support a native missionary evangelist for only $1,080 to $1,800 per year when my church says it takes more than $50,000 per year to support a Western missionary on the field?

ANSWER: There is a vast difference between living at the same level as an Asian peasant—as native evangelists do—and living at even a modest Western standard. In most of the nations in which we support local missionaries, they are able to survive on two to four dollars a day. In most cases, this is approximately the same per capita income of the people to whom they are ministering.

A Western missionary, however, is faced with many additional costs. These include international air transportation, shipping of many possessions to the field, language schools, special English-language schools for children and Western-style housing. Native missionaries, on the other hand, live in villages on the same level as others in the community whom they are seeking to reach for Christ.

The Western missionary also is faced with visa and other legal fees, costs of communication with donors, extra medical care, import duties and requirements to pay taxes in his home country. The cost of food can be very high, especially if the missionary entertains other Westerners, employs servants to cook or eats imported foods.

Frequently, host governments require foreign missionaries to meet special tax or reporting requirements, usually with payments required.

Clothing, such as shoes and imported Western garments, is costly. Many native missionaries choose to wear sandals and dress as the local people do.

For a Western missionary family with children, the pressure is intense to maintain a semblance of Western-style living. Frequently this is increased by peer pressure at private schools where other students are the sons and daughters of international businessmen and diplomats.

Finally, vacations and in-country travel or tourism are not considered essential by native missionaries as they are by most Westerners. The cost of imported English books, periodicals, records and tapes is also a big expense not part of the native missionary's lifestyle.

The result of all this is that Western missionaries often need 30 to 40 times more money for their support than does a native missionary.

QUESTION: It seems as if I am getting fund-raising appeals every day from good Christian organizations. How can I know who is genuine and really in the center of God's will?

ANSWER: Many Christians receive appeal letters each month from all kinds of religious organizations. Obviously, you cannot respond to all the appeals, so what criteria should you use to make your decision? Here are a few guidelines we have developed for mission giving, which I believe will help:

- Do those asking for money believe in the fundamental truths of God's Word, or are they theologically liberal? Any mission that seeks to carry out God's work must be totally committed to His Word. Is the group asking for money affiliated with liberal organizations that deny the truth of the Gospel, while keeping the name "Christian"? Do their members openly declare their beliefs? Too many today walk in a gray area, taking no stands and trying to offend as few as possible so they can get money from all, whether friends or enemies of the cross of Christ. The Word of God is being fulfilled in them: " . . . having a form of godliness, but denying the power thereof" (2 Timothy 3:5).

- Is the goal of their mission to win souls, or are they only social-gospel oriented? The liberal person believes man is basically good; therefore, all that is needed to solve his problems is to change his environment. One of the biggest lies the devil uses to send people to hell is, "How can we preach the Gospel to a man with an empty stomach?" However, the Bible says all—rich and poor—must repent and come to Christ or be lost. You must know which gospel is being preached by the mission group asking for your support.

- Is the mission organization financially accountable? Do they use the money for the purpose for which it was given? At Gospel for Asia every penny given for support of a missionary is sent to the field for that purpose. Our home office is supported with funds given for that purpose. Are their finances audited by independent auditors according to accepted procedures? Will they send an audited financial statement to anyone requesting it?

- Do members of the mission group live by faith or man's wisdom? God never changes His plan: "The just shall live by faith" (Galatians 3:11). When a mission continually sends out crisis appeals for its maintenance rather than for outreach, something is wrong with it. They seem to say,

"God made a commitment, but now He is in trouble, and we must help Him out of some tight spot." God makes no promises He cannot keep. If a mission group constantly begs and pleads for money, you need to ask if they are doing what God wants them to do. We believe we must wait upon God for His mind and do only what He leads us to do, instead of taking foolish steps of faith without His going before us. The end should never justify the means.

- Finally, a word of caution. Do not look for a reason for not giving to the work of God. Remember, we must give all we can, keeping only enough to meet our needs so the Gospel can be preached before " . . . the night cometh, when no man can work" (John 9:4). The problem for most is not that we give too much, but that we give too little. We live selfishly and store up treasures on this earth that will be destroyed soon, while precious souls die and go to hell.

QUESTION: How can I help sponsor a native missionary?
ANSWER: To help sponsor a native missionary through Gospel for Asia, all you need to do is the following:

- Visit Gospel for Asia online at www.gfa.org. Or call us at one of the national offices listed on page 227. Or write to Gospel for Asia using the tear-out coupon at the end of this book.

- Send in your first pledge payment. Most of our friends help sponsor missionaries for $30 a month.

- As soon as you receive information about your missionary, pray for him and his family every day.

- Each month as you continue supporting your missionary, we will send you a receipt for your gift. The lower portion of the receipt can be returned in the envelope provided to send in your next month's support. To keep costs to a minimum, we do not send monthly statements.

What Sponsors Say

"I believe that missions is one of the hardest things for Western Christians to relate to, because from our childhood we are raised to be materialistic and self-centered. This is not God's purpose! Our church's involvement with Gospel for Asia has done two dramatic things: First, our lifestyle has changed. We are now missions-conscious on a worldwide scale. Our people are getting beyond their own backyards. Second, we are more carefully examining each dollar we send for missions and asking, 'Is there waste involved here?' We support 60 native missionaries through Gospel for Asia, and the families here are having a chance to be connected with believers in the Two-Thirds World. They see their pictures, read their testimonies and pray for them. I am so very appreciative of our involvement with Gospel for Asia."

—Pastor L.B., Yuba City, California

"I was saved when I was 30 years old. My salvation experience was dramatic, and my life was turned completely around. I really feel that I know what it's like to be lost, and I have a tremendous burden for the unreached—those who have never heard about Jesus. When I found out about Gospel for Asia, I was so excited to know that I could play a significant part. I know that through my support thousands can come to know Jesus instead of slipping into hell. I rejoice to know that I am storming the gates of hell and impacting eternity."

—Miss J.F., Chicago, Illinois

"Our family has been quite involved in supporting native missionaries through Gospel for Asia (in fact, our kids each support one). We live in a small Midwestern town, and we've never really traveled much; so when the Lord brought this opportunity across our path, our perspectives really changed! We became less self-centered, our burden for the lost in unreached lands greatly increased, and we grew much more eternally minded. Now we are hungry to know more of the Lord's will for our lives. Our constant prayer is, 'Lord, use us. What more can we do for You?' "

—Mr. and Mrs. T.G. and family, Holdrege, Nebraska

Appendix Three

Contact Information

For more information contact the Gospel for Asia office nearest you.

UNITED STATES: 1800 Golden Trail Court
Carrollton, TX 75010
1-800-WIN-ASIA (1-800-946-2742)
info@gfa.org

CANADA: 245 King Street E.
Stoney Creek, ON L8G 1L9
1-888-WIN-ASIA (1-888-946-2742)
infocanada@gfa.org

GERMANY: Postfach 13 60
79603 Rheinfelden
(Baden)
07623-79 74 77
infogermany@gfa.org

UNITED KINGDOM: P.O. Box 166
York
YO10 5WA
01904-643-233
infouk@gfa.org

NEW ZEALAND: P.O. Box 302-580
North Harbour
Auckland 1330
0508-918-918 (Toll Free)
infonz@gfa.org

Notes

Chapter 4: I Walked in a Daze

1. Robert L. Heilbroner, *The Great Ascent: The Struggle for Economic Development in Our Time* (New York, NY: Harper & Row, 1963), pp. 33–36.

2. Economic Research Service, U.S.D.A., "Percent of Consumption Expenditures Spent on Food, 1999, by Selected Countries" (http://www.era.usda.gov/publications/sb965).

3. David B. Barrett and Todd M. Johnson, eds., *World Christian Trends, AD 30-AD 2200* (Pasadena, CA: William Carey Library, 2001), p. 417.

Chapter 5: A Nation Asleep in Bondage

1. Patrick Johnstone and Jason Mandryk, eds., *Operation World*, 21st century ed. (Carlisle, Cumbria, U.K.: Paternoster Lifestyle, 2001), p. 663.

2. Barrett and Johnson, *World Christian Trends, AD 30-AD 2200*, p. 44.

3. Rochunga Pudaite, *My Billion Bible Dream* (Nashville, TN: Thomas Nelson Publishers, 1982), p. 129.

4. Barrett and Johnson, *World Christian Trends, AD 30-AD 2200*, p. 421.

5. *Kingdom Radio Guide* (Holland, MI: Kingdom Radio Guide, Inc., 2003), p. 3.

6. Barrett and Johnson, *World Christian Trends, AD 30-AD 2200*, p. 45.

7. *Ibid.*, pp. 417–419.

8. *Ibid.*, p. 40.

9. *Ibid.*, p. 60.

Chapter 8: A New Day in Missions

1. Barrett and Johnson, *World Christian Trends, AD 30-AD 2200*, p. 416.

2. Charlotte Hails, "Christianity in China," Overseas Missionary Fellowship (http://www.us.omf.org/content.asp?id=27474).

3. Barrett and Johnson, *World Christian Trends, AD 30-AD 2200*, p. 426.

4. The World Bank, *World Development Report 2000/2001: Attacking Poverty* (New York, NY: Oxford University Press, 2001), pp. 21–24.

5. The World Bank, "World Development Indicators Database," April 2004 (http://www.worldbank.org/data/countrydata/countrydata.html).

Chapter 10: God Is Withholding Judgment

1. William McDonald, *True Discipleship* (Kansas City, KS: Walterick Publishers, 1975), p. 31.

2. A.W. Tozer, *The Pursuit of God* (Harrisburg, PA: Christian Publications, Inc., 1948), p. 28.

Chapter 11: Why Should I Make Waves?

1. C. Peter Wagner, *On the Crest of the Wave* (Ventura, CA: Regal Books, 1983), p. 150.

2. Watchman Nee, *Love Not the World* (Fort Washington, PA: CLC, 1968), pp. 23–24.

Chapter 12: Good Works and the Gospel

1. Barrett and Johnson, *World Christian Trends, AD 30-AD 2200*, p. 429.

2. A.W. Tozer, *Of God and Man* (Harrisburg, PA: Christian Publications, Inc., 1960), p. 35.

Chapter 13: Hope Has Many Names

1. Human Rights Watch, "The Small Hands of Slavery: Bonded Child Labor in India," (www.hrw.org/reports/1996/India3.htm).

Chapter 14: The Need for Revolution

1. C.S. Lewis, *The Problem of Pain* (London, U.K.: Fontana Publishers, 1957), pp. 106–107.

Chapter 15: The Real Culprit: Spiritual Darkness

1. Johnstone and Mandryk, *Operation World*, 21st century ed., p. 310.

2. Barrett and Johnson, *World Christian Trends, AD 30-AD 2200*, p. 428.

Chapter 16: Enemies of the Cross

1. Barrett and Johnson, *World Christian Trends, AD 30-AD 2200*, p. 32.

2. *Ibid.*, p. 655.

3. Johnstone and Mandryk, *Operation World*, 21st century ed., p. 310.

Chapter 17: The Water of Life in a Foreign Cup

1. Barrett and Johnson, *World Christian Trends, AD 30-AD 2200*, p. 655.

2. *Ibid.*, p. 40.

3. *Ibid.*, p. 61.

Chapter 18: A Global Vision

1. Dennis E. Clark, *The Third World and Mission* (Waco, TX: Word Books, 1971), p. 70.

2. "Understanding the Cost of Mission," Reformed Church in Missions (http://www.rca.org/mission/rcim/understanding.php).

3. Barrett and Johnson, *World Christian Trends, AD 30-AD 2200*, p. 655.

4. Roland Allen, *The Spontaneous Expansion of the Church* (Grand Rapids, MI: William B. Eerdmans, 1962), p. 19.

5. Barrett and Johnson, *World Christian Trends, AD 30-AD 2200*, p. 421.

Chapter 19: The Church's Primary Task

1. Barrett and Johnson, *World Christian Trends, AD 30-AD 2200*, p. 60.

2. George Verwer, *No Turning Back* (Wheaton, IL: Tyndale House Publishers, 1983), pp. 89–90.

Appendix 1: Questions and Answers

1. Barrett and Johnson, *World Christian Trends, AD 30-AD 2200*, p. 58.

SEND A NATIVE MISSIONARY TODAY!

I want to help native missionaries reach their own people for Jesus.

I understand that it takes from $90–$150† a month to fully support a native missionary, including family support and ministry expenses.

TO BEGIN SPONSORING TODAY,

visit our website at www.gfa.org

or call us in the US at 1-800-WIN-ASIA (1-800-946-2742)
Phone numbers for other national offices listed on page 227.

or fill out the form below and mail to the nearest GFA office.
National office addresses listed on page 227.

❑ Starting now, I will prayerfully help support _____ native missionaries at $30†† each per month = $_____ a month.

You'll receive a photo and testimony of each native missionary you help sponsor.

❑ Please send me more information about how to help sponsor a native missionary, including a one-year FREE subscription to *SEND!*—the voice of native missions.

Please circle: Mr. Mrs. Miss Rev.

Name

Address

City   State/PR/County   Zip/PC

Country   Phone (   )

E-mail

❑ Please send me free e-mail updates.   **CA51-RB1S   ZCV1-RB1S   YCV1-RB1S   3CV1-RB1S**

CHARTER
ECFA
MEMBER

A higher standard.
A higher purpose.

Gospel for Asia sends 100 percent of your missionary support to the mission field. Nothing is taken out for administrative expenses. All donations are tax deductible as allowed by law.

† CAN$120–$180, €45–€60, CHF 80–CHF 110, £50–£80, NZ$140–$240
†† CAN$30, €30, CHF 60, £20, NZ$40

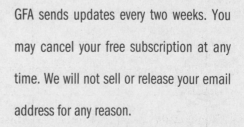

FREE subscription
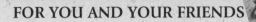

FOR YOU AND YOUR FRIENDS

Stay informed! Sign yourself, your relatives and Christian friends up for a FREE one-year subscription to *SEND!*, Gospel for Asia's quarterly magazine, featuring exciting and prayer-inspiring stories and updates from our native missionaries working in Asia. Simply fill out the form below for your free subscription.

Please circle: Mr. Mrs. Miss Rev.

Name

Address

City   State/PR/County   Zip/PC

Country   Phone ( )

E-mail

Please circle: Mr. Mrs. Miss Rev.

Name

Address

City   State/PR/County   Zip/PC

Country   Phone ( )

E-mail

CA51-PB1H   ZCV1-PB1H   YCV1-PB1H   3CV1-PB1H

Include additional names on a separate sheet of paper.

❑ Please identify me as the gift subscription donor.

My name is: _____

MAIL THIS FORM to one of Gospel for Asia's national offices listed on page 227.

OTHER MATERIALS FROM GOSPEL FOR ASIA

BOOKS BY K.P. YOHANNAN

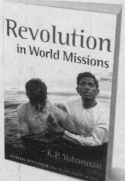

REVOLUTION IN WORLD MISSIONS

You've read it, now share it with a friend or family member!

Suggested donation: US $5 / CAN $5 / €3 / CHF 5 / £2.50 / NZ $8
Order code: **B1**

On audiocassette: US $10 / CAN $13 / €9 / CHF 14 / £5.50 / NZ $15
Order code: **B1AC**

AGAINST THE WIND

In this eye-opening book, K.P. Yohannan challenges you to consider how you are running the race God has set before you. Like the apostle Paul, you too can learn what it takes to be able to one day say, "I have fought the good fight; I have finished the race; I have kept the faith" no matter what the obstacles.

Suggested donation: **(HARDCOVER)**
US $15 / CAN $19.50 / €13 / CHF 20 / £10 / NZ $22.50
Order code: **B6**

THE ROAD TO REALITY

K.P. Yohannan gives an uncompromising call to live a life of simplicity to fulfill the Great Commission.

Suggested donation: US $10 / CAN $13 / €9 / CHF 14 / £5.50 / NZ $15
Order code: **B2**

On audiocassette: US $10 / CAN $13 / €9 / CHF 14 / £5.50 / NZ $15
Order code: **B2AC**

Order online at *www.gfa.org*

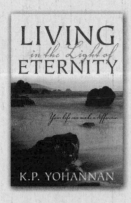

LIVING IN THE LIGHT OF ETERNITY

K.P. Yohannan lovingly, yet candidly, reminds Christians of their primary role while here on earth: harvesting souls. This book challenges us to look at our heart attitudes, motivation and our impact on eternity.

Suggested donation: US $10 / CAN $13 / €9 / CHF 14 / £5.50 / NZ $15
Order code: **B4**

On audiocassette: US $10 / CAN $13 / €9 / CHF 14 / £5.50 / NZ $15
Order code: **B4AC**

COME, LET'S REACH THE WORLD

How effective are the Church's current missions strategies? Are the unreached hearing the Gospel? K.P. Yohannan examines the traditional approach to missions—its under lying assumptions, history and fruit—in light of Scripture and the changing world scene. This book is a strong plea for the Body of Christ to partner with indigenous missionaries so that the whole world may hear.

Suggested donation: US $10 / CAN $13 / €9 / CHF 14 / £5.50 / NZ $15
Order code: **B3**

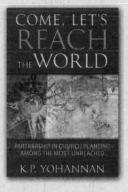

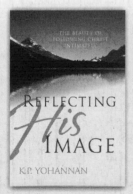

REFLECTING HIS IMAGE

K.P. Yohannan takes us on a journey back to God's original purpose for each of our lives: to reflect His image. This book is a compilation of short, easy-to-read chapters that all deal with following Christ closely.

Suggested donation: US $10 / CAN $13 / €9 / CHF 14 / £5.50 / NZ $15
Order code: **B5**

Order online at *www.gfa.org*

EXCITING VIDEOS AND DVDs

THE CALL TO HARVEST

In this 25-minute video, you'll meet the people who are near to the Father's heart: the unreached. See them through the eyes of native missionaries like Titus and Joseph, who face danger and hardship to preach the Gospel in Asia. As the life-giving presence of Jesus transforms lives and families daily, the Lord is calling His people everywhere to come and share the joy of this harvest.

Suggested donation: US $10 / CAN $13 / €9 / CHF 14 / £5.50 / NZ $15
DVD Order code: **DVD9**   *VHS Order code:* **V9**

CHRIST'S CALL: "FOLLOW MY FOOTSTEPS"

In this compelling 41-minute video, K.P. Yohannan challenges us to follow in Christ's footsteps—steps that will deliver us from our self-centeredness and cause us to impact the lost millions in our generation.

Suggested donation: US $10 / CAN $13 / €9 / CHF 14 / £5.50 / NZ $15
DVD Order code: **DVD1**   *VHS Order code:* **V1**

TO LIVE IS CHRIST!

Feel the passion of K.P. Yohannan as he describes the life-giving power of total commitment to Christ in this 55-minute video. Be amazed by stories of missionaries who risk their lives to preach the Gospel. Weep with him as he recalls his mother's years of sacrifice that changed lives for eternity. Many people search in vain for the path that leads to the abundant life that Jesus promised. K.P., through the Word of God, uncovers that path in this inspiring and challenging message.

Suggested donation: US $10 / CAN $13 / €9 / CHF 14 / £5.50 / NZ $15
DVD Order code: **DVD8**   *VHS Order code:* **V8**

Order online at *www.gfa.org*

JOURNEY WITH JESUS SERIES

VOLUME ONE

Living by Faith, Not By Sight (56 pp) — *Order code:* **BK1**
Journey with Jesus (56 pp) — *Order code:* **BK2**
That They All May Be One (56 pp) — *Order code:* **BK3**
Principles in Maintaining a Godly Organization (48 pp) — *Order code:* **BK4**
ALL FOUR BOOKLETS — *Order code:* **JBKS1**

SUGGESTED DONATIONS	**PER BOOKLET:**	US $3 / CAN $4 / €3 / CHF 5 / £1.50 / NZ $4.50
	PER VOLUME:	US $10 / CAN $12 / €10 / CHF 16 / £5 / NZ $16

VOLUME TWO

A Life of Balance (80 pp) — *Order code:* **BK5**
The Way of True Blessing (56 pp) — *Order code:* **BK6**
Seeing Him (48 pp) — *Order code:* **BK7**
Dependence Upon the Lord (48 pp) — *Order code:* **BK8**
ALL FOUR BOOKLETS — *Order code:* **JBKS2**

VOLUME THREE

The Lord's Work Done in the Lord's Way (72 pp) — *Order code:* **BK9**
The Beauty of Christ through Brokenness (72 pp) — *Order code:* **BK10**
Learning to Pray (64 pp) — *Order code:* **BK11**
Stay Encouraged (56 pp) — *Order code:* **BK12**
ALL FOUR BOOKLETS — *Order code:* **JBKS3**

Order online at *www.gfa.org*

ORDER

CODE	QUANTITY	DONATION
B2	1	$10.00
Your country's postage*:		
Additional donation:		
TOTAL DONATION ENCLOSED:		

US Postage: 10% of donation

German Postage: €4 (CHF 6) per order

New Zealand Postage: 1 item $1.80;
2–3 items $4.40; 4–5 items $5.70

Canadian Postage: 1–3 items $5;
4–8 items $6; 9–14 items $7;
15+ items add 25¢ per item

UK Postage: will be invoiced

Please circle: Mr. Mrs. Miss Rev.

Name

Address

City   State/PR/County   Zip/PC

Country   Phone ( )

E-mail

☐ Please send me free e-mail updates.   **CA51-PB1F**   **ZCV1-PB1F**   **YCV1-PB1F**   **3CV1-PB1F**

MAIL THIS FORM to one of Gospel for Asia's national offices listed on page 227.

Or visit us online: *www.gfa.org*

Make all checks payable to GOSPEL FOR ASIA. Please allow two to three weeks for delivery. All gifts are tax deductible less the fair market value of the materials you receive from us. The suggested donations are at or below the fair market value of each item and are subject to change.

A higher standard.
A higher purpose.